# Jeremy Harmer's 50 Communicative Activities

# Cambridge Handbooks for Language Teachers

This series, now with over 50 titles, offers practical ideas, techniques and activities for the teaching of English and other languages, providing inspiration for both teachers and trainers.

The Pocket Editions come in a handy, pocket-sized format and are crammed full of tips and ideas from experienced English language teaching professionals, to enrich your teaching practice.

Recent titles in this series:

# Jeremy Harmer's 50 Communicative Activities

Jeremy Harmer

Consultant and editor: Scott Thornbury

Shaftesbury Road, Cambridge CB2 8EA, United Kingdom

One Liberty Plaza, 20th Floor, New York, NY 10006, USA

477 Williamstown Road, Port Melbourne, VIC 3207, Australia

314–321, 3rd Floor, Plot 3, Splendor Forum, Jasola District Centre,
New Delhi – 110025, India

103 Penang Road, #05–06/07, Visioncrest Commercial, Singapore 238467

Cambridge University Press & Assessment is a department of the University of Cambridge.

We share the University's mission to contribute to society through the pursuit of
education, learning and research at the highest international levels of excellence.

www.cambridge.org
Information on this title: www.cambridge.org/9781009014120

First published 2022

20  19  18  17  16  15  14  13  12  11  10 9 8 7 6 5 4 3

Printed in Great Britain by CPI Group (UK) Ltd, Croydon CR0 4YY

A catalogue record for this publication is available from the British Library

ISBN 978-1-009-01412-0 Paperback
ISBN 978-1-009-01419-9 eBook

# Contents

# Thanks

This book wouldn't have happened if Scott Thornbury had not invited me to become part of such a lovely series. His attention to the material as it progressed, as with his contribution to our thinking about English language learning over the years, was as provoking and enjoyable as it was stimulating. I owe him a lot.

I was fortunate to move from Scott's interventions to the expert care of Karen Momber, a wonderful and challenging shepherd. I am grateful for her questions, her suggestions and above all her encouragement. Alison Sharpe edited 50 Communicative Activities with wonderful creativity and cheerfulness. The process was a pleasure.

Thank you Jo Timerick for enabling the whole thing with such grace and for keeping it all going.

It's been real fun putting this collection together with such expert guidance from such a great team. I feel very lucky.

# Acknowledgements

The authors and publishers acknowledge the following sources of copyright material and are grateful for the permissions granted. While every effort has been made, it has not always been possible to identify the sources of all the material used, or to trace all copyright holders. If any omissions are brought to our notice, we will be happy to include the appropriate acknowledgements on reprinting and in the next update to the digital edition, as applicable.

Text
Intro: Oxford University Press for the extract taken from Jeremy Harmer, *What is communicative?*, Apr 1982, Vol 36, Issue 3, by kind permission of Oxford University Press; Stephen L. Chew for the quote taken from 'How to Get the Most Out of Studying: Part 2 of 5'. Copyright © 2011 Stephen L. Chew. Reproduced with kind permission of Stephen L. Chew.

Typesetting
QBS Learning.

# Why I wrote this book

A long, long time ago I wrote an article in which I suggested that activities could be described as either communicative or non-communicative (Harmer, 1982). I wanted to separate activities, *per se*, from all the other noise surrounding what was being called 'The Communicative Approach' and I suggested that communicative activities had six characteristics:

- The learners have a desire to communicate.
- The activities have a communicative purpose.
- The emphasis is on content, not language form.
- Learners use a variety of language.
- There is no teacher intervention (e.g., correction).
- There is no materials control.

*Describe and draw*, where one learner had to tell another learner what to draw, was an early example of this, and story reconstruction (Harmer, 2015) where learners work out a story from different pictures they have separately seen, is another.

The opposite end of the spectrum, in my realisation, was occupied by activities with no communicative desire or purpose, where the emphasis was principally on language form, the teacher intervened (with correction, etc.) and the language was often material-dependent. Thus a Present simple 'presentation' with the sentences, 'She gets up at six o'clock. She has a shower. She drives to work. She works in a hospital,' etc. fits the 'non-communicative' moniker pretty well.

This way of looking at activities as either one thing (communicative) or the other (non-communicative), has permeated much of our thinking about communicative language teaching. As Beaumont and Chang (2011) argue, it has created a 'traditional/communicative dichotomy' in overall approaches to classroom procedures.

But not always. Some language teaching suggestions such as Task-based learning (TBL) or Task-based language teaching (TBLT) (Willis, 1996, Nunan, 2004) incorporated communicative activities/projects in a methodological approach/procedure. Meddings and Thornbury (2010) argued for learner-generated dialogic interaction and Zoltan Dörnyei (2015) proposes a 'principled communicative approach'– a kind of mix and match philosophy absorbing activities from both ends of the communication continuum. Even though none of these suggestions have been widely adopted, we might all accept that 'the main common denominator of communicative and task-based approaches in their various forms is that, even when they use form-focused procedures, they are always oriented towards communication' (Littlewood, 2004). However, I now think that those original six characteristics ignored other qualities which effective communicative activities can and should exemplify. Good communicative activities, I now suggest, are 'non-dichotomous' (see above) in that they wear both a learning-focus and a communicative face. They are effective as learning opportunities, even as the communication takes place. They share some or all of the following characteristics. They should:

- involve learners in deep processing;
- provoke purposeful repetition;
- encourage learners to process language for meaning, not just form;
- provoke learners to give attention to, and make connections between, the language they encounter and the context/discourse where it occurs;
- provoke interaction between the learners' language processing and the texts and stories they are engaged with; *and*
- provoke communication between learners and promote group cohesion.

From Hyde and Jenkins (1969) and Craik and Lockhart (1972), to Chew (2011) and Kosslyn (2021), psychologists have argued that *deep processing* – where language is processed for meaning, context and, crucially, emotion – is better for memory retention than *shallow processing* – where language is only processed for its properties – how it is spelt or pronounced, for example. Nattinger (1988) quoted experts who argue, as Curran (1976) did, that people learn a language best when they have a strong personal stake or 'investment' in it. Chew claims, extravagantly, that with deep processing, people 'learn whether they want to or not.' However plausible this piece of old research strikes you as being, the underlying principle that we learn best when we are both emotionally and cognitively engaged is one that seems to me to be crucial to successful learning.

Repetition has always been beneficial for language learning. Claire Kramsch, for example, has suggested, 'utterances repeated are also utterances resignified' (2009). I gloss 'resignified' as 'given new or newly nuanced meaning.' Meaning-lite habit-forming drills by themselves may not let this resignification happen though, because they may fail to 'allow for the human mind in learning, of consciousness, thought and unconscious mental processes' (Hall, 2011). What a good activity needs, then, is *purposeful* repetition where the human mind *is* involved in learning.

A good activity will get learners to focus on meaning, not just on form. When they choose the words and phrases they wish to interact with or use, they should be doing so consciously so that effective learning takes place.

Good communicative activities encourage learners to give attention to the language they encounter and relate it to the context it occurs in – as well as allow them to see how it relates to other items of language around it. Thus, if learners come across a naturally-occurring lexical phrase in a powerful story they experience, for example, they will get information about when and where such a phrase can be used – which will help them when they come to use it themselves.

Finally – and typically – a good communicative activity will provoke communication between learners and promote group cohesion for, as so many commentators have argued over the years, 'success depends less on materials, techniques and linguistic analyses, and more on what goes on inside and between the people in the classroom' (Stevick, 1980).

In many ways effective communicative activities exemplify the characteristics of what Merrill Swain called 'the comprehensible output hypothesis' (e.g., Swain and Lapkin, 1995) where teachers 'push' learners to speak or write in the target language.

Not all the activities in this book necessarily prioritise spoken English with learner-learner interaction, however. It is my contention that an individual learner's own internal *intra*personal engagement and interactions with language can, and rightly should, be included in what gives an activity both learning and communication potential as well as the *inter*personal face-to-face interactions which are normally the ones described.

### How this book works

Activities are grouped into six categories: *Engaging communication*, where the learners' enthusiastic participation is the main driving principle; *Practising communicatively*, that slightly uneasy blend of language practice and free speaking; *Interacting with text*, because we communicate 'about' something; *Making decisions*, because negotiation is a crucial part of communication; *Presenting and performing things*, because speaking, in particular, is often a kind of performance; and *Activities in sequence*, showing how communicative activities can fit in with other things. Most of the activities hover around the A2–B2 level – I will comment where this might be problematic and make suggestions – or even higher, where the communication inevitably becomes more extensive. They are for any age, just about, though topic and sophistication will limit some of them, of course. I detail a procedure for using each activity and give examples. I then say why it 'works for me' as a communicative activity before suggesting alternatives.

The Coronavirus pandemic – and the extended lockdown quarantines it necessitated – provoked a renewed interest in, and practice of, online instruction. Accordingly, where appropriate, suggestions for online adaptation are given.

It is worth reiterating that the activities in this book do not constitute a method. However, they share an underlying core belief that language is learnt best through emotional, cognitive and human engagement.

The publications/videos I have referenced are below. They represent a mix of work that varies in its level of 'academica' and as such represent the kind of range of opinions which influence the practice of English language teaching.

# References

Beaumont, M. and Chang, K-S. (2011). 'Challenging the traditional/communicative dichotomy.' *ELT Journal*, 65(3), 291–299.

Chew, S. (2011). 'How to get the most out of studying Part 2.' Retrieved from https://www.youtube.com/watch?v=9O7y7XEC66M&list=PL5JLlM7WjW5X5wbqgmahuhIL7jT5_psiU&index=3 Accessed 19/11/2019

Craik, F. I. M. and Lockhart, R. S. (1972). 'Levels of processing: A framework for memory research.' *Journal of Verbal Learning and Verbal Behavior*, 11, 671–684.

Curran, C. A. (1976). *Counseling-learning in second languages*. Apple River Press.

Dörnyei, Z. (2015). *The Principled Communicative Approach*. Helbling Languages.

Hall, G. (2011). *Exploring English Language Teaching*. Routledge.

Harmer, J. (1982). 'What is communicative?' *ELT Journal*, 36(3), 164–168.

Harmer, J. (2015). *The Practice of English Language Teaching: Fifth edition*. Harlow, Essex: Pearson Education Limited.

Hyde, T. S. and Jenkins, J. J. (1969). 'Differential effects of incidental tasks on the organization of recall of a list of highly associated words.' *Journal of Experimental Psychology*, 82(3), 472–481.

Kosslyn, S. M. (2021). *Active Learning Online*. Alinea Learning.

Kramsch, C. (2009). *The Multilingual Subject*. Oxford: Oxford University Press.

Littlewood, W. (2004). 'The Task-based approach: some questions and suggestions.' *ELT Journal*, 58(4), 319–326.

Meddings, L. and Thornbury, S. (2010). *Teaching Unplugged*. Peaslake: DELTA Publishing.

Nattinger, J. (1988). 'Some current trends in vocabulary teaching' in Carter, R. and McCarthy, M. *Vocabulary and Language Teaching*. Cambridge: Cambridge University Press.

Nunan, D. (2004). *Task-Based Language Teaching*. Cambridge: Cambridge University Press.

Stevick, E. (1980). *Teaching Languages, A Way and Ways*. Heinle & Heinle Publishers.

Swain, M. and Lapkin, S. (1995). 'Problems in Output and the Cognitive Processes they generate: A Step Towards Second Language Learning.' *Applied Linguistics*, 16(3), 371–391.

Willis, J. (1996). *A Framework for Task-Based Learning*. Harlow, Essex: Pearson Education Limited.

# A: Engaging communication

Activities in this section are designed to provoke enthusiastic engagement in the process of communication whilst, at the same time, ensuring some focus on the language being used. They are intended to make learners as comfortable as possible with the creative use of English.

**Everybody up**

> Learners stand up and, where possible, move to the centre
> of the room. They are organised in small groups of about
> five. They discuss topics suggested by the teacher or by
> themselves so they can report on their conversations later.

*Everybody up* is a term I have borrowed from Jane Revell (2015 and
elsewhere). It is, of course, similar to other 'walkaround' activities such
as *Find someone who* and other 'mingle' suggestions.

1  Ask all the learners to stand up and move the furniture so that there
   is a space in the middle of the room.
2  Separate learners into small groups – from three to seven people. Tell
   them that they should complete the following task:

   *Find out who in the group plays or played a musical instrument.*
   *Find out why they started and if they still play. If so, find out how*
   *often and where they play, how often they practise and how they*
   *learnt. If no one in the group plays a musical instrument, find out*
   *what instrument they would like to play and why.*

   (Harmer and Revell, 2015)

   Tell learners that you will be asking for a report from some of the
   group members when the task is over. While they are doing the
   activity, move around monitoring them, making sure that they are
   on task. Be available to help with words and phrases they need,
   if necessary.
3  If possible, make a space so that the next stage of the activity takes
   place whilst everyone is standing up – it makes listening more
   'immediate' and active. Ask a representative to tell the rest of the
   class about the musicians – or would-be musicians – in the group.
   When this is done, invite everyone in the class to ask the people they
   have heard about any more questions.

4   Get members of each group to tell you what they learnt. Use what has been said as an opportunity to focus on some of the language you heard, pointing out where things could have been said differently or better.

## Why it works for me

Because learners move into a different 'space' and work in small groups rather than, say, pairs, the activity modifies the usual pattern of the lesson and provokes a very life-like communication atmosphere and experience. This activity is genuinely communicative in a content, language and very human way.

## Alternatives

I chose the topic of music – playing a musical instrument – because almost anyone can relate to it, musician or not. Nearly all non-instrumentalists wish they could play music in some form, and most are more than happy to talk about it. But, of course, there are many other topics like this – ones with universal human appeal. We could substitute sport, signature dishes that people cook, hobbies we have, places we regularly visit, people's attitudes to the names they were given, etc. The main thing to have in mind is that we want learners to talk about areas of universal interest.

## Online/virtual variations

Using a 'hands up' protocol (previously agreed with the class) where people indicate when they want to speak/ask a question, learners can interview each other. But that doesn't match the advantages of the face-to-face version. Better, maybe, to put learners in breakout rooms in groups and have them report back after a set time.

Harmer, J. and Revell, J. (2015). *Jetstream Intermediate Student's Book*. Helbling Languages.

## 2    Personal interviews

Students interview each other based on questions that are suggested by an initial learner contribution.

Personal interviews are especially appropriate at the beginning of a new semester with new learners. At the A1 level they can be as simple as having learners ask, 'What is your name?' 'Do you have a pet? What is its name?' 'What is your favourite food?' However, the version I am going to use is more like a B2 level activity and closely follows one described by Rachael Roberts (see the reference below) as, 'one of my favourite speaking activities because it is flexible and can be used at any level'. The beauty of it is that after a short stimulus from the teacher, it is the learners who make all the language and meanings.

1   Think of a few questions (say ten) about yourself which you would be happy to answer in public.

   *Where do you live?*
   *Who – if anyone – lives with you?*
   *Do you have any pets and if so, what are they?*
   *What's your favourite thing in the house/apartment?*
   *Or for a higher level:*
   *What is the scariest thing you have ever done?*
   *Who would you most like to meet and what would you say to them?*
   *What music would you like to hear/did you hear at your wedding?*

   Then write the answers to your questions on the board (without telling the learners what the questions were).

2   Learners now work in groups to try and work out what the questions might be for the answers on the board (see also **12**). While they are doing this, go round the room helping them with language problems, etc. But again, do not confirm what the questions were.

3   Now learners get into pairs and use the questions they have come up with in stage 2 to interview each other. They do this in turns.

4   Learners can now either tell the class about their partner or they can write a short paragraph about them which might go up on the classroom wall.

## Why it works for me

What do some people like talking about best? Themselves! And as a genuine piece of communication – especially at the beginning of a course – this has to be included here. Couple that with attention to language and its predictable interactions and this classic activity has its place in any effective teacher's repertoire.

## Alternatives

Klippel (1984) has an activity called *Identity cards* where learners have to fill in a form about their partner and then tell the class about them. She suggests the task can be varied by not using cards and saying instead, 'Find out three things about your partner that are important or interesting,' or 'Find out five things about your partner that one could not find out just by looking.'

We can add a playful element by having learners pretend to be someone else (a celebrity, a historical figure, etc.) and the interviewer has to find out who they are.

There is a much more extensive job-based interview sequence in **49**.

## Online/virtual variations

This activity works perfectly well in an online context with a little bit of adaptation. We can share the screen to show learners the answers to our own questions (see stage 1 above) or we could put the answers in the chat box. We can then discuss with all the learners on the screen what the questions might be. If we can – and if it is not too organisationally complicated – we then put the learners in pairs. If that doesn't seem plausible then we can have the class interview one learner after another. We will have to manage the conversations well – who speaks next, etc.

Klippel, F. (1984). *Keep Talking*. Cambridge: Cambridge University Press.

Roberts, R. https://www.teachingenglish.org.uk/blogs/rachael-roberts/rachael-roberts-a-favourite-speaking-activity. Accessed 02/02/2021

**Space station speed dating**

> Learners have to choose who they want to accompany
> them for their year in a space station hovering above
> the earth.

In the USA in the 19$^{th}$ century, there was a custom where women,
looking for a husband, would invite eligible young bachelors on
1$^{st}$ January for fifteen-minute-maximum visits. Was that the origin
of speed dating in which couples try and see if there might be any
attraction and compatibility between them in structured three-minute
interviews?

ELT classrooms should not be dating environments (!), though Laura
Hayward uses an enjoyable activity of this kind on the video to
accompany Harmer (2007), but the short, structured interview is a
naturally effective communicative activity at almost any level and age.

1  Tell learners that they are going to spend a year in a space station
   400 kilometres above the earth. They will take one person with
   them. They have to choose who that is.
2  Discuss ideal qualities for a companion in such circumstances. What
   kind of character should they have? What would make them easy
   to live with and reliable in the event of trouble? What should they
   be good at? The language of the questions will obviously depend on
   the level of the group. Prompt learners with suggestions to try and
   broaden the discussion.
3  Now ask learners to write a maximum of four questions (that's all
   there will be time for) to help them work out who their ideal space
   station companion is. This is not a romantic speed dating activity –
   it's more practical than that! They do this individually. While they
   are working on their questions, go round the class helping learners
   with language suggestions.
4  Tell learners they are about to start the procedure and that they will
   have a maximum of two minutes to interview each 'candidate'.

5 Learners now form 'fluency circles' (Bohike, 2013) where half the class stand in an inner circle facing outwards and the other half form an outer circle facing inwards. The outer circle learners must interview the inner circle learners opposite them. They should have notebooks with them to record their thoughts.

6 The interviews start. After two minutes (or three, if you think that is necessary) ask the outer circle learners to move one person to the left. Now they interview the new learners in front of them.

7 When the circle has been completed, it is now the inner circle's task to interview the people opposite *them*. As before, they have two (or three) minutes for each interview.

8 When the activity is over, have a discussion with the class. Who would they choose and why? Which of their questions were the most effective? How useful have they found the activity, etc? This is the moment where you can clear up any language issues that may have arisen.

## Why it works for me

Learners work together, building inter-group cohesion. They have to make a choice and this demands deep processing. There is purposeful repetition, obviously. The activity is dynamic and fast-moving.

## Alternatives

Some teachers do actually role play a speed dating session (with no need for a space station!), but it has to be done in an appropriately light-hearted way (see also 2 and 48).

## Online/virtual variations

It would be difficult to create fluency circles online. However, we can create an interview panel for a space station team. Groups (the whole group, or groups in breakout rooms) can design their questions and then interview members of the other groups one by one (with everyone looking on). With smaller classes we wouldn't need to form breakout groups, of course.

Bohike, D. (2013). 'Fluency-oriented second language teaching' in Celce-Murcia, M., Brinton, D. M. and Snow, M. A. (Eds). *Teaching English as a Second or Foreign Language: Fouth Edition*. Heinle Cengage Learning.

Harmer, J. (2015). *The Practice of English Language Teaching: Fifth edition*. Harlow, Essex: Pearson Education Limited.

**Experts**

> Learners pretend to be experts in a subject. They have to
> answer questions put to them, but only one word at a time.

Many years ago, I saw this activity being demonstrated by Ken Wilson
at a teachers' conference and was instantly impressed by it. All of
the class are involved in this activity either as the 'experts' or as the
'journalists'. The role of the teacher is to create the setting and then to
keep the pace moving along, because that's part of the fun.

1 Tell the class that they are extremely lucky to have world experts
  with them – in this case people with world expertise on bears (the
  animals). They can ask the experts anything they want and they will
  know the answer. Learners understand that they are about to play
  some kind of a game.
2 Ask the learners to think of questions they would like to ask world
  experts about bears: 'How dangerous are they?' 'What makes them
  angry?' 'What do you do if you meet a bear?' etc. They can discuss
  this in pairs.
3 Ask half the class to stand at the front of the class in a line facing
  their classmates. They are the bear experts! Say that when they are
  asked a question, they have to answer one word at a time along the
  line. When they get to the end of the line they double back. They
  have to keep each sentence going for as long as they can!
4 If this is the first time you have used this activity, do a demonstration
  round. You can ask the experts your own question – anything will
  do! – such as, 'How tall are bears?' Start at the beginning of the
  line and get learners to say a word – probably 'bears'. Now indicate
  the second person in the line who might say 'are'; then the third
  learner could say 'sometimes'; the next learner might say 'very';
  then the next learner 'tall'; the next learner might say 'but'; the next
  learner might say 'some' etc. so that the sentence goes something
  like this: 'Bears are sometimes very tall but some bears are shorter

than that and some are fat but some are thin ...' It may not be very enlightening, but it is good fun, and best of all it makes learners think of what words are both grammatically and semantically possible.

5  Now ask one of the journalists to ask a question and once again get the experts to answer one word at a time. As before, your role is to push the sentence along giving encouragement where learners are having trouble thinking of a word – offer them suggestions when they get stuck.

6  After two or three rounds, swap the journalists and the experts around and now the new journalists ask the new experts *their* questions.

**Why this works for me**

By making speaking aloud into a game – where participants are not judged for their attempts at fluency – reluctant speakers will feel more comfortable, we hope. This is vital if we want to encourage them to attempt fluent conversation later. They have to process deeply to make the right grammatical/lexical choices in a hurry.

**Alternatives**

Any activity/game in which learners have to speak one word at a time in sequence will work well. For example, learners might have to construct a letter one word at a time (in pairs or groups) or make a speech.

**Online/virtual variations**

Given the latency issues of most online connections, this activity will have to be slower with deft use of the mute button and learners numbered in advance! They can be trained for that. The game also works well as a written game where learners can key their words into the chat box.

## 5    What's my line?

In groups, learners prepare to talk about (and mime) what
people in various different jobs do in their working lives.
They are interviewed by other groups who have to guess
what the occupation is.

*What's my line?* was a TV show which ran in the USA from
1950–1967 (and in the UK until 1996). This adaptation works well in
language classrooms.

1   Tell learners to imagine that they have a particular job – anything
    from being an astronaut or a costume-designer, to an ice-skater, a
    nurse or a train driver. Later, others will interview them to try and
    guess what their occupation is.
2   Put learners in groups of equal numbers to choose an occupation – as
    many groups as is feasible, depending on the size of the class. They
    must then discuss what people in that occupation do: exactly what
    processes they use, what they do when they start their working day
    and what routines are typical. The group lists all these things.
3   Learners in the group now try and describe these things without
    being absolutely clear about what they mean! For example, if they
    wear a nurse's uniform they can say 'special clothes' instead. If they
    use a stethoscope the learners can say, 'I always carry a special piece
    of equipment with me,' etc. They also dream up some mime activities
    (see also **40** and the rest of Section E) they could do to represent
    the occupation.
4   When the groups have finished their preparation, a learner from
    each group goes to another group. They do their mimes to the
    group they have gone to. The group they are miming to discuss for
    a maximum of 45 seconds what they think the occupation is before
    making a decision and writing it down. The visiting learner does not
    say if they are correct.
5   Groups now interview the visiting learner for a maximum of two
    minutes. They cannot ask, 'What is your occupation?' or 'Do you

drive trains?' but they can ask less direct questions such as 'Why do you do your job?' or 'How many hours a day do you work?' 'What time do you start work?' The visiting learner must answer truthfully (whilst using their imagination) but try not to give the game away.

6  At the end of two minutes the group votes on what they think the occupation is. The visiting learner now says if they are correct. The group gets five points if they choose the correct occupation and an extra five points if that is the same as their vote after the mime.

7  Visiting learners now go back to their original groups. A different learner from each group goes to visit a new group (different from the one their original group visited) and the procedure is repeated – and again the points are recorded (see stage 6 above). Repeat the procedure until all the learners have been a visitor to a group.

8  During all the previous stages, monitor the groups, help out with procedural matters if things get stuck, and keep a record of particular language problems. When the activity is finished, find out which group scored the most points, bring successful language you have heard to everyone's attention and discuss any language problems that can be solved there and then or need to be worked on later.

## Why it works for me

Its initial discussion phase, the voting and the questioning give the whole activity real communicative purpose. It is fun, there is (some) movement, there is a lot of enjoyable repetition, etc.

## Alternatives

Visiting learners can pretend to be a famous person. They can visit a doctor with an imaginary – ridiculous – ailment (i.e., she thinks she's a giraffe!) or go to a job interview (he thinks he's a secret agent).

## Online/virtual variations

This is an ideal game for online teaching. Depending on the size of the group, the 'visitor' can prepare alone (though this loses part of the activity's function) and/or we can use breakout rooms, just as in a face-to-face classroom.

## 6 Portrait interviews

Learners interview/interrogate people in famous paintings and photographs. The portraits talk to each other!

Teachers are always looking for ways to motivate learners to use language communicatively, and especially to ask questions and listen attentively to the answers so they can continue the conversation accordingly. I first encountered this activity in Cranmer (1996) in which he used *The Arnolfini Marriage* (Jan van Eyck, 1434). Learners even asked the dog in the picture some questions!

1 Ask learners if they know of any famous portraits (such as *The Mona Lisa*, *Girl with a Pearl Earring*, *The Arnolfini Marriage*, *Self-Portrait* by Vincent van Gogh, or Picasso's *Portrait of Dora Maar*). You might want to ask them why they think people paint portraits, and why people have their portraits painted. They can write sentences about this (which will make them less self-conscious when they answer).

2 Show learners three different portraits (you can choose your favourites or put something like "famous portraits" into an online search engine to find ones that are appropriate for this activity). Ask them to choose who they would most like to interview. When they have chosen, ask them to think of questions they could ask the portrait. Explain that they can ask about anything from (for example), 'Where did you get that earring?' to 'What do you have for breakfast?' or 'Why do you look unhappy?' Learners can create their questions individually or in pairs (or even brainstorm in groups).

3 Now ask learners to look at the portrait again and try to imagine how the person there might answer some of the questions that have been suggested.

4 To demonstrate the activity, choose one of the more confident learners and ask them to pretend to be the person in the portrait. Say that they should answer the questions as if they were that person in whatever way they think is appropriate, thinking carefully

about how their portrait would respond. Help the learner along with suggestions but don't over correct. Stress to the learners who ask questions that they should ask a follow-up question based on how their first question is answered. If a questioning learner can ask more than one follow-up question, that's even better!

5   Repeat the activity with one or two other learners. As always, stress the importance of following up the 'portrait's' first answer with follow-up questions.

6   Learners can now practise their interviews in pairs while you go round helping them out and offering suggestions.

7   The interviews present a fantastic opportunity to showcase successful language or communication that you have heard learners use. You can ask some pairs to perform their conversations to the rest of the class. Suggest alternatives to language that hasn't worked quite so well.

## Why this works for me

This role play activity (see also 27 and 28) works because it is fun; because it allows learners to be imaginative without putting them on the spot – so helping them on the way to becoming confident speakers – because learners are encouraged to process language for meaning and have to communicate with each other.

## Alternatives

I remember a booklet produced for primary teachers who were going to take their classes to the Fitzwilliam Museum in Cambridge, many years ago. There were lots of ideas including my favourite: 'What do the gallery portraits say to each other at night when the doors are closed and the lights go out?' Alternatively, learners can interview celebrities, etc.

## Online/virtual variations

We could screenshare the portrait in question and then have learners think up questions in pairs or groups. We could then select which learners role play which character and interview them on the screen.

Cranmer, D. (1996). *Motivating High Level Learners*. Harlow, Essex: Longman.

**Musical stories**

> Learners create stories together using music to guide their characters and images.

Educators have long recognised the power of music to provoke and stimulate creativity. Most people have an innate ability to recognise the difference between sad and happy music, and between threatening and romantic music, for example. The mood in most movie scenes is established through music as well as image. Filmmakers can make any conversation romantic, threatening or ordinary by changing the music that accompanies it! This activity is built around that fact and is based on a procedure outlined by Keegan (2012). See also Cranmer and Laroy (1993).

1 Students are in four groups. Each group gets a different piece of music to respond to (you can use/bring in pre-prepared tracks or have learners access the music you have chosen on their devices). The only two characteristics you need to ensure is that (a) it suggests a strong mood of some kind and (b) it is instrumental (i.e., without words). Ideally it should last for between one and three minutes only.

2 Ask one group to use the music to conjure up a person. Are they male or female? Are they kind or unkind, selfish or generous, etc? (You can seed the activity with characteristics like this to guide learners' thinking.) Ask another group (who listens to a different piece of music) to conjure up their own person in the same way. Ask the third group to imagine a location based on the different music they are listening to. Is it inside or outside? What's the weather like? How warm is it, etc? And ask the fourth group to say what their music makes them think of. Does it suggest love or hate, peace or war, movement or stillness, happiness or sadness, etc?

3 Now make new groups of four with one learner from each of the original groups. Tell learners to create a film scene between the two people (who two of the learners have imagined), in a setting that one learner's previous group described, about the topic that the fourth learner brings along.

4 Now tell learners to write a short dialogue reflecting the scene they have imagined.
5 Learners now act out their dialogues for the class. Encourage the other learners to give constructive feedback. You can add your own suggestions about what they might do differently.

## Why this works for me

Like many (but not all) others, I am constantly overwhelmed by music's power to evoke response and images. We are opening learners' communicative brains to non-linguistic stimuli to provoke precisely the kind of language and content attention that we hope for in inter-group communication.

## Alternatives

A writing activity that I have often described and used (Harmer, 2015) involves the same kind of use of music to stimulate learner creativity. Dictate a sentence to the class. (My favourite is, 'She turned and looked at him.') We then play learners some music with a strong 'mood' to guide their writing of a short story. We tell them to 'write what the music tells you'. The process is repeated with the same opening sentence, but with a piece of contrasting mood music. Learners swap their stories with a partner who reads out one of the stories they have in front of them. The rest of the class have to guess which piece of music it was written to.

## Online/virtual variations

We can do the same activity online using different breakout rooms – or other ways of regrouping the class. We can refer different learners to different online music resources and by giving them a time limit we can try to ensure that they don't get lost in their musical explorations.

Cranmer, D. and Laroy, C. (1993). *Musical Openings: Using Music in the Language Classroom*. Harlow, Essex: Pearson Education Limited.

Harmer, J. (2015). *The Practice of English Language Teaching: Fifth edition*. Harlow, Essex: Pearson Education Limited.

Keegan, P. (2012). 'Musical storytelling.' *English Teaching Professional*, 79.

## 8 Fishbowl improvisation

> Learners have to continue conversations with words and phrases that are suddenly put into those conversations.

Rather in the same way as *Experts* (4), this activity – which has been around for a long time – can have a very positive effect on learners' confidence. I'm going to adapt a procedure used by Philip Harmer (personal communication) which mixes the original activity with an end-of-the-week vocabulary review. We can do this with the whole class or – for more participation and less 'risk of exposure' for participants – learners can be put in small groups.

1 Ask learners, individually, to write three to five words or phrases they have learnt recently on separate pieces of paper.
2 Collect all the words and put them in a bowl (the 'fishbowl' – or a hat or a box or some other container). Put the fishbowl in a place which is easy to reach.
3 Introduce topics for discussion which will be easy for learners to speak about – especially things which have relevance in their lives and circumstances, and which are appropriate for their age and level. For example, we can ask whether people should be allowed to download music for free, if judges should be chosen by political parties, if people should be allowed to own guns, if exams should be abolished, if the voting age should be lowered, if primary teachers should be paid more than university teachers, if men should do 50 percent of the housework, etc. or some very quick fire topics like 'Cats or dogs?' 'Early morning or late night?' 'Formal dress or informal dress?, 'High heels or flat shoes?' etc.
4 Learners start the conversation after a minute or two to collect their thoughts. And they go round the class/group giving their opinion which must reference something that a previous speaker has said (much like *Tennis match* – 16). At certain points, direct a learner who is about to speak to reach inside the bowl and pick out a piece of paper. As immediately as possible, they must incorporate what

is on their piece of paper into what they are saying. It has to make sense! The discussion then continues until the next time a learner is directed to pick out a piece of paper and the process is repeated.

5  While the activity is taking place, do not intervene unless you absolutely have to. But when it is over, you can clear up any language difficulties that may have arisen and make suggestions about how to say things better.

**Why it works for me**

Talk about making learners relate language in context! As with **4**, the game-like nature of this communicative activity takes the pressure off learners. They are supported in their attempt to meet a challenge, not judged for their lack of fluency. Everyone understands how challenging this is!

**Alternatives**

A more game-like activity modifies *Fishbowl* to be more like the children's birthday activity *Pass the parcel*. The bowl is passed round the circle, learner by learner. It stops when we give a signal (or when the music stops). The learner picks out a word/phrase and instantly has to start speaking about something, using the word or phrase they have.

*Fishbowl* can be played as a team game. When a member from team A uses one of their words correctly, they get a point.

We can turn *Fishbowl* words and phrases into screen prompts. Now every time we put a new word or phrase up on the screen, learners have to incorporate it into their conversation.

**Online/virtual variations**

This works well with the 'screen prompt' option (see above). We can share the screen – obviously – or we can have everyone open the chat box and put the words there.

## 9 Wordless conversation

> Learners try and enact dialogues using only sounds and gestures.

It may be strange to find this activity in a book about communication – after all it doesn't initially involve the use of too many words. Except of course that it does! I first experienced this activity (and realised its potential) at a workshop run by Paula Wilson in the UAE some years ago.

1 Tell learners that they are going to make conversations in pairs, but not in the normal way.

2 Have a discussion with the class to decide what the conversation should be about, and other details. Have learners give you (a) a place where the conversation takes place, (b) who the two people are (i.e., a police officer, a chef, etc.) and (c) what the topic of the conversation is.

3 Now put the learners in pairs. Tell them to create a short dialogue – six exchanges maximum. Ideally, they should write down what they come up with, but the main thing is to plan the conversation and learn it.

4 Now get the pairs to think of how they will say the dialogue – and in this case more importantly – how they will use their tone of voice and gestures, etc. to make the conversation more communicative.

5 Now tell learners that they are going to have the same conversation again, but this time without using actual words. In order to do this, they have to use sounds, nonsense words, gestures and expressions to get their meanings across.

6 Now a pair stands up and performs their conversation for the rest of the class who have to try and guess what they are actually saying. They tell the learners what they think is going on and the pair (who can now use words!) says whether they are right or wrong. If no one has got anywhere near what they were trying to convey, they try again. And once again the other learners try to work out, and then suggest, what happened in the conversation.

7 Finally, the pair re-does their conversation, only this time they use actual words. Give (and encourage the other learners to give) feedback and, maybe, suggest better ways of saying things.
8 The class can choose which they think is the best conversation. Finally, each pair has to work together using that conversation and do their own version of it.

## Why it works for me

This activity makes learners think about ways we communicate in speech, quite apart from the words we use. It makes learners process language in their own heads both as interpreters and performers. But I like it especially because it challenges learners in an imaginative and different way.

## Alternatives

We could have only one learner in a pair use nonsense words – or sounds rather than words. Now the class's task is somewhat easier since they only have one speaker to 'decipher'.

A slightly different activity is to give learners a dialogue to act out (or they construct a dialogue themselves) using real words, but then secretly hand each participant a piece of paper with something written on it such as 'speak angrily' or 'speak sadly'. The other learners have to guess the adverb – which makes them concentrate on what they are listening to, but also on how it is being said.

## Online/virtual variations

This activity is quite difficult to do online in the same way. So much depends on gesture, expression and voice tone. However, it *is* do-able and by using the breakout rooms the same thing can be achieved, but instead of having the other learners make their suggestions of what they are hearing out loud, they can write them up in the chat/text box to get round some of the mute/unmute problems which we often encounter with online speaking.

**Drawing happy dreams**

> Learners draw their thoughts and the other learners have
> to try and guess what it is they have drawn.

There is a long tradition of asking learners to visualise scenes, silently,
in their heads (especially when teachers want them to focus on the
present continuous or descriptions, etc.). For example, we can ask them
to imagine a beach scene in their heads and write down who they can
see doing what: 'Two children are playing with a beach ball,' etc. They
can listen to what we tell them with their eyes closed and then try to
remember what we said. This example, heavily based on Clare and Marsh
(2020), uses the same basic idea to create a reason for communication.

1   You can start by asking learners if they dream often, if they
    remember their dreams when they wake up and what they think
    dreams do and are for.
2   Give learners a number of sentence prompts and ask them to
    complete them about their experiences. Here are three examples:

    *Dreams are the brain's way of ...*
    *My dreams are most vivid when ...*
    *A repeating dream I seem to have is ...*

3   Learners share their sentences in groups or pairs and expand – if
    they want to – on their answers to the questions in stage 1. While
    they are doing this, circulate and help out with language suggestions
    where that seems appropriate. When they have finished, ask them to
    share their discussions with the class.
4   Now ask learners to close their eyes and think of what a happy
    dream would be like for them – or a happy dream they remember
    having. Where are they? Who is in their dream? What happens?
    When they wake up, how does it make them feel?
5   The learners now open their eyes, and individually they draw
    anything they can about the dream they have been thinking of.
    Their pictures don't have to be accurate (a lot of people don't
    draw particularly well!). They can just draw basic shapes or details

from the dream. Of course, learners may mess around with the activity and invent things, but provided it is creatively done and not transgressive, that is OK.

6 Learners now give their drawings to a partner – without saying what it represents. Their partner tries to make sense of it.

7 Now pairs tell each other what they think their partner's drawing represents.

8 Learners now discuss at least two similarities and two differences between what they think they have seen in each other's drawing (see also **18**). At this stage they have not told each other what their drawings *really* represented.

9 Finally each learner explains what their pictures were actually meant to show!

## Why it works for me

Language is not just for functional interaction; it is also a means of expressing images and thoughts (and dreams). That's what this activity reminds us of. And by sharing these, we help learners to develop the ability to communicate such images.

## Alternatives

We can ask learners to visualise almost any scenario – such as their favourite sport, leisure activity, food, etc. Anything that they can properly visualise will work here. We could also turn the whole thing into a role play – where housemates meet in the kitchen and one starts a conversation with, 'I've just had the weirdest dream ...'

## Online/virtual variations

This activity can easily be done online if learners either have a camera or can share their screens. One learner can show their pictures and the others in the group can try to interpret it. We could also put learners into breakout rooms, although that might be a bit cumbersome to organise. It would be important to work out clear rules for how and when learners take turns, etc.

Clare, A. and Marsh, A. (2020). *The Creative Teacher's Compendium*. Pavilion Publishers.

**Mystery objects**

Learners introduce mystery objects and their classmates have to try and work out what they are through initiating information-seeking conversations.

During the pandemic isolation, business companies worried that their usual welcoming procedures for new employees wouldn't work in a virtual environment. No welcoming coffee chat, no physical office tour, no personal connection. But of course, we can meet online, and one way to help people introduce themselves has been to partially show something in their office or their house/flat and either describe it or ask people to speculate what it might be. Such partial showing is a perfect springboard to communication.

1  Take something unusual into class and conceal it in a bag or paper so that its shape is visible, but without the detail for the learners to know definitively what it is. It can be anything from a ball of wool to a device for quickly re-stringing a guitar; from a sculpture of a horse to a child's pair of shoes.

2  The learners now have to ask you questions to try and work out what it is. Learners can only ask a *yes/no* question ('Is it a …?') when they are guessing the object's identity. Your job is to answer truthfully, whilst not giving the game away too easily.

3  When learners have found out what the object is (or have got as close to guessing correctly as they are likely to get), show them the object and get them to ask you questions about where you got it, why you like it, what it is used for, etc. Encourage learners to ask you more questions about it and let them see it close up if they want to.

4  When it is over, you can discuss the kinds of questions that work and which don't work – and you can further get learners to tell you the loose rules of the activity: 1 the more mysterious the better, 2 the questions they can/cannot ask, 3 answer truthfully but not

100 percent transparently (the effectiveness will depend on level of course), 4 be ready to say more about the object when the activity finishes.

5 Now that learners have enjoyed the activity, tell them to come back to the next class with something they wish to show in the same way. Make sure they know how to say it in English, and if they want, they can research English ways of describing it online.

6 Learners then share their mystery objects either in pairs, groups or with the whole class. You can prompt with suggestions and encouragement, but as with all communicative activities, don't focus too rigorously on absolute accuracy.

## Why it works for me

You couldn't ask for a better example of deep processing than this attempt to work out what someone is showing you (or telling you about). It creates group cohesion and involves meaning and language processing.

## Alternatives

Just as online companies welcome employees by allowing them to share partial photographs, so we can have learners bring in photographs of unfamiliar objects – or ask them to photograph things which are unusual. The activity then proceeds as before.

A simplified version of this activity is the radio game *Twenty questions* where learners can also only ask *yes/no* questions – a maximum of twenty. As in that game we can turn our activity into a competition by setting time limits or limits on the number of questions, etc. That may possibly make it more motivating but reduces its communicative 'reach'.

## Online/virtual variations

This activity works beautifully online – as the example from the business world above suggests. Objects, mystery photographs, etc. can be shown or demonstrated.

## 12 Discussion cards

Learners are given a series of random discussion questions. Together they explore their opinions and their answers to those questions.

What creates the best discussion in an ELT classroom? Is it the staged debate (46), the adversarial *Tennis match* (16), or something as easy to organise as this discussion game (included, incidentally, in Thornbury, 2005)? True, we know that it is very difficult to offer instantaneous opinions in a foreign language unless you possess significant ease with that language, but with our encouragement, prompting and support, learners will do their best to give it a go.

1 Tell learners that they are going to have discussions and that they will have to speak instantaneously when they are asked to.
2 Put learners in groups and give each group one of the following topics (you can choose different topics depending on your group):

*Regulations and laws*
*Appropriate behaviour and appearance*
*Places to live*
*Wealth and poverty*
*Education and school*
*Art and artistic expression*

3 Tell the group to think of a number of debatable questions for the topic they have chosen. For example, for the topic 'regulations and laws' it could be anything from, 'Does punishment actually work?' 'Is the death penalty ever acceptable?' 'Should we punish public (graffiti) artists, and how?' to 'Is it (should it be) a crime to make jokes about mothers-in-law?' The linguistic sophistication of the questions will depend on the level of the learners. You can offer suggestions and corrections for the questions they are designing.
4 Learners now write their questions on separate pieces of paper and give them to you. Put them in a hat or bowl or some other container where they are mixed up (see also 8).

5   Take the container back to the groups and without looking they choose five cards. They look at the topics. They can reject up to two cards if they don't like the topic and choose two more. They then discuss these. While they are doing this, go round offering help and suggestions.

6   When sufficient time has elapsed, learners can report back on the discussions they had. Open up discussion on what appears to have been interesting topics with the whole class.

## Why it works for me

The necessary characteristics for effective communicative activities (deep processing, group cohesion, processing for meaning as well as form, etc) which we identified in 'Why I wrote this book' on page ix are clearly in evidence here. On top of that, this activity is also very time-efficient for the teacher and not dependent on massive preparation or materials. Perfect!

## Alternatives

The discussion activity can be done with the whole class, although group work is probably preferable since learners are less challenged by having everyone listen to them (with the whole group).

We can have the groups finish by selecting the best one or two questions from the ones they have been discussing. We now write six of these questions on the board where the whole class can see them. We can reformulate the questions to make them less ambiguous – more transparent. We could spend a bit of time having learners think and talk about the questions – a kind of 'topic and lexical warm up'.

In groups, a learner throws a dice, and then, depending on what number comes up, they discuss the question which they can see on the board for that same number.

## Online/virtual variations

It is possible to replicate all this by putting learners into breakout rooms online. The activity proceeds as before, but this time all the questions go in the chat box (or on a shared screen). We can either put them back into groups or have the whole class discuss – but ensuring that everyone allows others to take turns, and that everyone has a chance to give opinions. We can have learners choose the best five questions for discussion.

Thornbury, S. (2005). *How to Teach Speaking*. Harlow, Essex: Pearson Education.

**House rules**

> Learners discuss different rules for parts and rooms of
> their house.

Adapted from Johnson and Rinvolucri (2010), this activity asks learners
to share their own internal house rules. Different cultures and learners
have their own rules!

1 Ask learners to think about their homes and picture them in their
  heads, silently. Now ask them to have a think about what rules there
  are in their house: are people expected to take their shoes off when
  they enter the house/apartment? What else is normal behaviour?
2 Draw a floorplan of the downstairs of a house on the board – one
  that shows where the furniture is, windows, doors etc. and ask them
  to draw two floorplans of the downstairs of their house.
3 Now have learners think about what happens when they walk into
  the house. (Shoes? Where do people put their coats? What happens
  next?) They should put a number – on one of the plans – next to any
  regular procedure. Putting numbers there is an aide-memoire (just
  like the Cuisenaire rods in 22) for future recall.
4 Now get learners to write down any rules they can think of about
  what happens in their house/apartment. For example, 'That chair
  is where Dad sits.' 'All plates go in the dishwasher.' 'Guests must
  not do the washing up unless they are asked.' 'Don't touch musical
  instruments unless invited,' etc. When learners have finished, they
  should write a number on the plan to remind them of those rules.
5 In pairs, each learner gives their second plan (which they haven't
  written on) to their partner. They tell their partner about their rules
  and the partner writes in the numbers as they are told about them
  and asks questions to make sure they have it all clear in their heads.
  The process is repeated.
6 Learners now combine into groups of four. They share what their
  partner told them about their house rules. The groups discuss the

similarities and differences between the rules in different houses. How many rules are shared between all houses? How many only exist in one house?

7   While this is going on, keep an eye on what is being said – only intervene if appropriate or necessary.

8   Now the class discusses the activity. What surprised them? How similar were people's rules? You can point out successful and less successful uses of language.

## Why it works for me

This activity involves learners in deep processing – the topic demands it! Everyone understands what it is about and will have something to say. There will be lots of purposeful repetition and, hopefully, some genuine (and surprising?) real life information.

## Alternatives

Instead of house rules, learners can discuss school rules, or the rules of societies/groups they belong to or sports they play, for example. If younger learners are going on an exchange visit, they can contact host families on this topic, Johnson and Rinvolucri suggest.

## Online/virtual variations

Estate agents who want you to buy a property often include virtual video tours in their online brochures. We can get learners to make their own videos – if they are comfortable with this – and give a running commentary as they go around the house.

Johnson, G. and Rinvolucri, M. (2010). *Culture in our classrooms: Teaching language through cultural content*. DELTA Publishing.

# B: Practising communicatively

Activities in this section feature language practice – in other words they incorporate a focus on the language itself. They are very familiar but are given a communicative edge – i.e., they involve deep processing (see 'Why I wrote this book' on page ix) to make learners more engaged with what they should be learning.

> Learners have to ask questions which get exactly the answer –
> from another learner – that is written on their card.

Asking questions is a vital ingredient in conversation – whether out of genuine interest, a need to get information or understand, a desire to discover the truth, or an attempt to know someone better. All questions provoke a variety of possible answers, but if we ask the 'right' question we can find out exactly what we want! This *Ask the right question* was one of the first activities to come out of what was then the brand 'new' Communicative Approach.

1  Tell learners that the object of the game is to focus on asking exactly, and precisely, the right question to get exactly the right answer.
2  Demonstrate the activity to show how it works. For example, write up the following five words or phrases on the board:

*mosquitoes    11 in the morning    violin    zucchini    red*

3  Tell learners they have to ask questions and you will reply with what is written on the board only if they ask exactly the question you are thinking of for that answer – or which forces you to give that answer. Questions like, 'What animals cause disease?' could be answered in a number of ways whereas for, 'What animals kill the most humans in the world every year?' the answer must be, 'Mosquitoes.'
4  Learners start asking the questions, which you answer truthfully (if you want to!), but only answer if they ask a question to which your words or phrases are perfect answers. For example, if learners ask, 'What green vegetable do many people eat?' you could well say 'There are many, including broccoli, peas, peppers, courgettes, etc.' But it is only if they ask a question like, 'What is the American name for courgette and small marrow?' that they will definitely get the answer, 'Zucchini.'
5  Now ask a learner up to the front of the class. Tell them that they can only answer questions from the class if the answer which

the questions provoke exactly matches the words which are on the board. Help them and encourage them – and be prepared to explain why a question that has been asked is not exactly fit for purpose.

6 Now either give learners a list of words or ask them to write their own words in order to do the same activity. If they work in pairs or groups, more learners will have a chance to speak and listen in a more relaxed setting than as the whole class. While they are doing the activity, you can go round the class helping and offering suggestions.

## Why it works for me

This activity may look like a vocabulary game, but it demands a degree of language processing which has significant cognitive payoff. Learners have to pay equal attention to meanings and linguistic precision. They really have to listen to each other – so it provokes group interaction and cohesion.

## Alternatives

We can model a five-pointed star activity where each star point has a word or phrase written on it which represents something in a life (e.g., *Brussels*, *three*, etc.) and the learners have to find the right questions to get those answers, e.g., 'Where were you born?' 'How many guitars do you have?' etc.

Learners read a text and do some comprehension work on it. Give them some words and phrases from the text. They now have to ask exactly the right questions to get one of those words or phrases. This makes learners interact with meaning in the text and context and forces them to think really carefully about the information they find there.

## Online/virtual variations

This activity is relatively easy to do online. Teachers can message individual learners with their word and that learner then has to answer the questions the others ask them on screen. As before, they can only answer if the question exactly provokes the word they have been given as the answer.

> Learners have to guess a word or phrase they cannot see based on what their classmates are telling them.

It may seem odd to have a vocabulary review game included in a collection of communicative activities, but it is here because its built-in information gap can only be closed by communication, and learners have to find creative ways of paraphrasing the vocabulary behind the learner 'victim'. At A1 level, the degree of communication will not be high with this (or any other) game. But with higher levels it becomes more sophisticated and involves more complex paraphrasing. You can see the teacher Louise Russell doing this activity on the video which accompanies Harmer (2007).

Though there is no conversational interaction of a social kind, nevertheless we should remember that communication comes in many forms, even games!

1   Divide the class into two teams – or more if it is a big class. Each team must select one of their members to be the first 'victim'. Place a chair for each team facing the class (i.e., with its back to the board).
2   The first 'victims' sit in the chairs. Write a word or phrase on the board (from a previous lesson or lessons) behind the seated learners. Their teams have to describe the word or phrase. For example, if (at A1 level) the word was *running* they might say, 'When you walk very fast but not walking.' The instructions are quite clear: learners may not use physical gesture or any other acting technique. And it goes without saying that they can't say what the word or phrase is or use any form of the word in their definitions.
3   The first 'victim' to answer correctly gets a point for their team.
4   Now each team selects another of their number, and you write another word or phrase on the board.
5   The game continues with different learners taking turns sitting in the chairs. Keep it going until just before you sense the fun is about

to go out of it. If you wish, you can go on to have learners use the words they encountered in the game in some other way.

## Why it works for me

As with the previous activity, *Backs to the board*, although it is a game, nevertheless demands cognitive and emotional engagement. Added to that, it is competitive and good fun! Hopefully, one team isn't ridiculously better than the other.

## Alternatives

We don't have to use the board; we can hold up cards which the selected individuals cannot see.

A popular party activity which achieves the same kind of communicative game playing is the identity guessing game *Who am I?* In this game, learners decide on well-known people from contemporary life or history. They write the names on separate pieces of paper (ideally, post-its or other slightly sticky notes). These are then affixed to other learners' foreheads. Their job is to find out who they are by asking *yes/no* questions. Depending on the level and age of the learners, these can range from the obvious, 'Am I alive?' 'Am I a man?' to more complex ones such as, 'Am I the kind of person you would like to meet?' (They are not, of course, allowed to ask, 'Am I a man or a woman?' since that demands an answer more than 'yes' or 'no'.) How long will it take them to find out who they are?

## Online/virtual variations

We can play this game online by having the selected individuals turn their backs on the screen and we show the words or phrases that have been selected to the others so that they can answer that individual's questions. Alternatively, they can choose the words and the teacher can be the one who has to guess.

---

Harmer, J. (2007). *How to Teach English: Second edition.* Harlow, Essex: Pearson Education Limited.

Learners throw opposing opinions at each other, team to team – like playing a game of tennis, in a way!

One of the most difficult things for learners in a foreign language is to have a proper discussion where they can offer disagreement. Part of the reason for this is that they need time to think about what they want to say – automaticity (a key component of fluency) takes time, repeated exposure and practice. This activity, then, gives learners that crucial thinking time. Years ago, Luke Prodromou (1995) suggested a similar batting of opinions backwards and forwards to make exam practice more agreeable.

1 Tell the learners that you are going to ask them to come up with arguments both in favour of a proposition and against that same proposition. Offer them a choice between a number of topics such as, 'Air travel should be discouraged,' 'Tourism is good for communities,' 'Social media is good for society,' 'Vegetarianism should be made obligatory'.

2 When learners have chosen the topic, divide the class into two groups. One group should come up with as many arguments in favour of the proposition as possible. The other group does the opposite, of course, and thinks of reasons why the proposition is a bad idea. While they are doing this, you can go round the groups offering suggestions and language help. Group members can ask you for words and phrases which would be useful.

3 Now explain that when someone from one of the groups (say, Group A) gives an opinion, someone from Group B should counter that opinion, like a game of tennis, where people exchange shots over the net. Now someone else from team A counters that 'shot' with their own 'volley'. Keep the pace going. If learners in a team cannot decide who should take the shot, nominate one of them to speak next. It should be stressed that you do not want to encourage

learners to read out sentences of statements, but rather to speak more spontaneously.

4 When the activity has continued for as long as it can while still being engaging, draw it to an end. This is an ideal moment to highlight particularly successful interventions from learners. You can suggest alternative ways of saying things and draw attention to any especially common problem areas.

5 Now dissolve the teams. Once again, give learners some thinking time while they work out which of the arguments they found especially sympathetic to their own feelings on the topic. This can then lead to a general discussion on the topic they have been discussing, only this time they have a chance to express what they themselves really think.

(For an extended, more formal, version of this activity, see **46**.)

**Why it works for me**

This is an enjoyable and relatively easy way of getting learners used to a 'for and against' way of doing discussions. It's fun and encourages group 'togetherness'. There is purposeful repetition of content and language.

**Alternatives**

We can 'seed' the activity with a few 'jokers'. These are learners who, no matter what team they are on, can give their own opinions at crucial stages of the activity. We can nominate one of the jokers if the conversation gets bogged down.

**Online/virtual variations**

Learners could prepare their 'for and against' arguments in two different breakout groups. We then play the game in the same way as face-to-face, but participants will have to abide by our nomination protocols, or alternatively, we can nominate which learners should speak next. This will make the activity less spontaneous, of course, but it is perhaps the best we can do!

Prodromou, L. (1995). 'The Backwash effect: From testing to teaching.' *ELT Journal*, 49(1), 13–25.

# Learner-generated drill chains

> Learners create their own stories during a structure-focused grammar drill.

This activity, which demands no preparation or materials, has been around forever, it seems. I had almost forgotten it until, a few years ago when I was filming short interviews with teachers about successful lessons they had taught, I met a young woman called Andreea Draghici in Bucharest, Romania who described how she had used it. Her sense of satisfaction at the learners' stories created with drill chains was infectious.

Instead of having to repeat sentences from a situation which she would normally introduce – in the usual PPP model (presentation, practice and production) – or from a coursebook, for example, learners created and expanded their own story.

In the following example (different from the specific one that Andreea used) we will focus on the first conditional.

1  Tell learners that there is a woman who is paddling out to sea on a surfboard.
2  Ask learners to complete the following sentence, 'If she goes too far out, she won't ...' Maybe one of them will say, 'She won't be able to get back to the beach.'
3  Now ask learners to make the whole sentence, 'If she goes too far out, she won't be able to get back to the beach.' Then get learners to say, 'If she can't get back to the beach, she will ...' and maybe a learner says something like 'she will try and see a boat'. The learners gradually understand that the next sentence – using the same grammatical pattern – must start with the last half of the previous sentence, e.g., 'If she sees a boat ...'
4  However serious or silly the story turns out to be, it will be the learners who create it. Meanwhile, your role is to help them make well-formed sentences and/or to help them find vocabulary they need.

5  When learners finish one of the stories or simply run out of ideas, you can either conduct a short language analysis session or offer a new situation and start the whole process again – though this time with a different story.

## Why it works for me

Why are we discussing what is, after all, a grammar lesson in a book of communicative activities? Because learner-generated chain drills provoke meaningful 'resignified' repetition as well as meaningful interaction between members of a group. They demand processing at the level of language and of meaning. This activity clearly has enough effective communicative elements to be included here.

## Alternatives

The most obvious variations in the activity we have described so far are content and language; we can create, for example, a situation of someone missing their train to work in the morning; of a child getting lost in a city; or a farmer whose crops are failing; of someone whose car breaks down in the middle of nowhere; of someone who has won or come into a lot of money – and so on and so on. The possibilities are endless.

We can change the language focus, too. We could, for example, use this kind of drill chain activity with past forms (past simple, past perfect). A woman found herself stranded on a desert island. What did she do? (1) She made a hut. (2) After she had made a hut, she went for a swim. (3) After she had gone for a swim, she … etc. Indeed, any language-focused drill can be used in this way.

## Online/virtual variations

We can do this easily enough online. All we have to do is to nominate individual learners to speak next from the ones who are there on our screens. Alternatively, we can get them to do the drill in the chatbox and we can insert our comments there – or use the screensharing possibilities available for whatever program we are using.

Learners talk to each other, usually in pairs, to identify
the differences and similarities between, for example, two
different paintings or buildings or objects.

An activity that was first described by Dick Allwright (1976) and which
has stood the test of time, is called *Find the differences* with, also, its
sibling *Find the similarities*. This activity combines both and provides
learners with a proper reason for communication.

In the example below, I use two paintings by the artist Marc Chagall (*At
Night* and *Bouquet with Flying Lovers*).

1  Put learners in pairs or groups (see online variations below). Give
   each learner or group a picture and tell them to study it. At this
   point they don't share their picture – or any thoughts about it – with
   their partner. Tell learners to think of how to say exactly what is in
   the picture, what the colours are (unless you give them black and
   white pictures) and where things are. This will be important in order
   to find things that are similar and different. For example, in both
   of the Chagall paintings there is a couple – but whereabouts in the
   pictures, exactly, are they? What is in the sky? And what is on the
   ground below? Is it day or night? And so on. (You might want to
   prepare for the activity by making sure learners can say things like
   'on the left/right,' 'in the top right-hand corner,' 'in the middle of the
   picture,' 'at the bottom of the picture,' etc.)
2  When learners have had a chance to study their pictures, they start
   to discuss them with their partner – without showing their picture
   to the person they are working with. Thus, they rely entirely on each
   other's description of what they have been looking at.
3  You can add an extra level of challenge by setting a time limit for the
   activity (say three minutes maximum).
4  When the activity is over, ask how many similarities and differences
   the learners found and get them to tell the rest of the class. See who
   found the most.

5 Now ask learners to show each other their pictures – or project them so that everyone can see them. Ask them what they think now! This will be a good opportunity to discuss any language that has come up or which you wish to suggest.

## Why it works for me

I like this activity because it demands observation and concentration from the learners. It is easy to organise for teachers. The competitive element – who can find the most similarities/differences – gives it a slight kick, too!

## Alternatives

We don't have to use paintings, of course. Similar photographs or cartoons will do just as well. Learners could each read different poems, interpret their meanings and then do an *Everybody up* exercise (see **1**) to find things which are the same or different about them. We must choose poems which are appropriate for the learners and the level they are at (see **42**).

## Online/virtual variations

We can do this kind of activity online, although it is more difficult over the airwaves to provoke spontaneous conversation. There will be pauses! But that should not stop us – or our learners. We can start by dividing the class into two groups (A and B). In their different breakout rooms, we show them their individual pictures and they can discuss (in their groups) what they see. Now we can either pair learners off (which is quite complex), or have the group discuss on screen – or in the chat/text box – what the similarities and differences are.

---

Allwright, R. (1976). 'Language learning through communication practice.' *ELT Documents*, 76(3).

# Truth and lies 19

Learners prepare a number of statements about themselves at least one of which is false. The other learners have to guess which the false statement is.

*Truth and lies* is often used to practise language items that learners have previously focused on. This example is based on a lesson on video by Juan Pablo Monfón Jiménez (Pablo) in Mexico (see Harmer, 2015), though the activity predates that lesson by many years! However, the really communicative aspect of this mini-sequence comes when learners try out their own true and false sentences and others discuss which of the sentences they believe. (For longer communicative sequences see Section F.)

1  Tell the learners a (hopefully) motivating story. Ask some questions to check their comprehension and then give them other tasks to ensure their understanding of what they have heard – in Pablo's lesson, learners had to put pictures in order to reflect the sequence of the story he had just told them.

2  Ask learners to find examples of particular language use. In the case of Pablo's lesson, they had to notice examples of *get/got to*: identify *get* + adjective (*got lost, got desperate*), *get* + noun (*got a sandwich, got a phone call*) and *get* + adverb (*got home, get around*), etc.

3  Up to this point the lesson looks like a listening and grammar activity and not appropriate for a communicative activity book! But now ask learners to think of five statements about themselves (using the target structure). Three of them should be true but two of them should be false so that at stage 4, communication can take place.

4  Learners take turns to tell the rest of the class their statements. The class decides if they are true or false, giving reasons in the case of the latter. The author of the statements then reveals the truth.

5  Other learners can question a learner's truths and lies further to get more information from them so that conversation opens up.

6   While the activity is going on, give feedback and gentle correction (where you may intervene, lightly, to help the communication along).

At various stages, Pablo, in common with some other teachers I have observed, uses the timer on his phone to be exact about the time limit he sets for some of the stages of this activity – unlike the sometimes inexact and unrealistic times we suggest and enact!

## Why it works for me

As with **17**, this activity is very engaging for learners because they create the content, which is both emotionally and cognitively engaging.

## Alternatives

We can ask learners to tell stories with untruths in them. There is a wonderful TV programme in the UK called *Would I lie to you?* where a guest is given a statement they haven't seen before about themselves (i.e., 'I once destroyed by mother's best dress by burning it on the cooker.') and they have to instantly invent a story and withstand questions from their colleagues before they (the colleagues) decide if it is true or a lie. Good fun.

## Online/virtual variations

*Truth and lies* is easily adaptable if we are teaching online. We need to establish how and when learners say their statements and how and when the others are chosen to comment. We might use in-built program symbols, or make gestures, to say which statements they think are lies. We can mix speaking and the chatbox to make things clear.

Harmer, J. (2015). *The Practice of English Language Teaching: Fifth edition.* Harlow, Essex: Pearson Education Limited.

> Learners have to justify their opinions on a controversial topic by adopting certain 'positions' and explaining their views and why they hold them.

*Four corners* relies on the jigsaw procedure (see **25, 26**) to provoke mental processing and involves valuable task repetition (see Bygate, 2018). Our example will focus on one of the most popular sports in the world: football.

1 Tell the learners that they are going to discuss the world of football. Lead a discussion about some of the issues in football – how important it is, whether there's too much money around it (for clubs and players), how important it is in a nation's life, whether learners are at all interested in it, etc.

2 While the discussion is going on, note down any strong arguments that might be worth investigating and then write four of them (or ones that you have pre-prepared) on the board. Here are four possibilities (but you and your learners will probably come up with much better ones):

- *Some people say football is more important than life and death; actually, it's more important than that.* (Often attributed, somewhat carelessly, to Liverpool manager Bill Shankly.)
- *Footballers are paid far too much money.*
- *Local clubs should only have local players in their teams.*
- *Too much attention is given to football in the media.*

3 Let the class discuss these opinions and try and elicit arguments in favour of each one. Ask them to vote on the one they like the best.

4 Now write each opinion on a separate piece of paper and put them at the four corners of the room. Ask learners to go and stand with the opinion that they most agree with. You need at least two learners for each opinion. Tell them to discuss (again) the arguments in favour of the statement.

5 Now one person from each statement moves in a clockwise direction to the next corner. They ask the people who are there to justify their opinion and they challenge them with as many questions as they can. After two or three minutes these same people move again to the next opinion and the procedure is repeated. When the activity has finished, ask learners (the ones who moved) if they want to change their corners. Now the process starts over with a different 'traveller'.

6 Continue the activity until you sense that the learners' engagement is about to fade.

7 While the activity is progressing, circulate and help out with suggestions when and if things get a bit stuck.

## Why it works for me

I love the mixture of ideas, movement, physical space and repeated language and content. A rich mix indeed, this activity exemplifies everything we ask for from an effective communicative activity.

## Alternatives

The same kind of effect occurs if we create a line with extremes at either end (i.e., 'boxing should be banned – boxing is a great sport'). Learners have to stand on the place in the line which represents their view, and then have to justify it to their colleagues. Does anyone move as the discussion progresses?

## Online/virtual variations

We can use a quadrant (a horizontal line intersected with a vertical one) activity. The ends of the horizontal axis say, 'Football is really important' and 'Football is nothing more than a game'. The ends of the horizontal axis say, 'Footballers are paid too much money' and 'Footballers should be allowed to earn what they can'. Learners can draw the diagram and put a cross in the diagram to show where they 'stand'. They hold their diagrams up to the camera to show them (or share their screens). The others can question them either orally or write their questions/comments for the 'presenter' to read.

Bygate, M. (2018). *Learning Language through Task repetition*. John Benjamins Publishing Company.

Learners use different pictures to make a story using an information gap technique.

This is one of the most iconic of first-generation communicative tasks. As with *Jigsaw reading*, it relies on creating an information gap (see **25**). This activity, however, uses pictures, not words, to create the need for communication. I have used this technique countless times both in class and in course materials.

1   Divide the class into four groups (or five or six depending on the number of pictures you have). Each group has a letter A–D.

2   Each of the four groups gets a separate picture. The pictures I am going to describe come from one of the first examples of this technique I ever encountered as a beginning teacher (Holden and Byrne, 1978). Picture number 1 (in no sequential order) shows two nurses looking in surprise at an empty (previously occupied) hospital bed. Picture number 2 shows an elderly man with a walking stick in a dressing gown standing at a pedestrian crossing pressing the control for the traffic lights. Picture 3 shows a paramedic helping an elderly man with a walking stick to get into an ambulance. Picture 4 shows an elderly man in a dressing gown talking energetically to a young police officer who is making notes in her notebook.

3   Tell the groups to study the picture they have in front of them. They should try and work out exactly what is going on and think of all the words and phrases they can use to describe what seems to be happening.

4   Take the pictures away from the groups. Now make new groups. Each new group has a learner from the original group A, one from group B, one from group C and one from group D. Tell learners to describe their pictures to each other from memory, explaining exactly what was going on in their pictures.

5   Now tell the learners to try and reconstruct the story which the pictures tell. While they are doing this, you can go round the groups

listening and helping out. Don't tell them what (you think) the story is, but help them with any language difficulties they may be having.

6   Now ask the learners to tell their stories to the rest of the class. Don't say what the correct story is (partly because there isn't one, and also because that any version that makes sense is entirely OK!). The class can vote on the best story. When the activity has finished, you can draw the learners' attention to things that went well and maybe suggest (or invite learners to suggest) alternatives to things that didn't go so well.

## Why it works for me

When learners go to their new groups, they take with them language they have already rehearsed with the original group and it is their responsibility to transmit that and the content it describes. Then they have to communicate with each other. A lovely virtuous circle.

## Alternatives

Any picture sequence will do, provided it has the potential to tell a story. There is nothing to worry about if the sequence is somewhat ambiguous. That will provoke more discussion.

We can merge this activity with other media. Thus, one group could see a picture/photograph, another group could look at some newspaper headlines, another group could listen to some music, etc. They then combine these sources to try and piece together a story.

## Online/virtual variations

We can make this activity work online by sending different learners to different breakout rooms – or by using the 'close your eyes' technique (see **10**). They can then conduct their discussions in the breakout rooms.

Holden, S. and Byrne, D. (1978). *Follow it through*. Longman.

Learners use Cuisenaire rods (or pictures, etc.) to describe where they live and are questioned by other learners to build a group description.

Described by Earl Stevick (1980) and named after the city where he first used it, *Islamabad* uses Cuisenaire rods (small wooden blocks of different sizes and colours, originally designed for maths teaching – see below). Islamabad was, for Stevick, a Community Language Learning (CLL) activity.

Bill Harris reminded me about the activity (private communication). Nick Bilbrough's account (2011) and his reflections many years later (Bilbrough, 2014) give a lot more information. The version here emphasises communication between learners.

1   Learners are told to think about the neighbourhood they live in and how they would describe it. If more than one learner lives in exactly the same area, then they should choose their grandparents' neighbourhood, or somewhere they used to live, or a holiday place, etc. What happens there? What doesn't happen there? What does it look like? Who and what do they see around them? What's the atmosphere like? They can visualise this if you ask them to close their eyes before asking them these questions and any others you can come up with (see 10).

2   Learners now make quick notes about what they have visualised. Ask them to think about how they would describe their neighbourhood so that other people in the class can understand them. They shouldn't write down whole sentences, but in the time you give them (two to four minutes), they should silently try out what they are going to say in their own heads.

3   Put learners in small groups of, say, five learners (see Alternatives below for whole-class versions of this activity). One learner now takes the Cuisenaire rods and uses them, one by one, for each piece of information about their neighbourhood which they tell the others. When they have finished, other learners in the group

point to/hold up one of the rods and describe (in their own words) what it represents and what their group member said.

4   When everyone has 'remembered' the original learner's description, he or she corrects/amends some of the mis-remembered summaries. The group now questions the original learner to find out more and clarify details.

5   Repeat the procedure (stages 3 and 4) with each of the other learners in the group. While this is going on, go round the groups listening and offering constructive feedback, only when it seems appropriate.

6   At the end of the activity, learners from one group ask learners from another group to describe some of the neighbourhoods they have heard about. They can ask questions about them.

## Why it works for me

This exemplifies the idea of deep processing which we discussed in 'Why I wrote this book' on page ix. The responsibility of describing something you care about cannot be overestimated!

## Alternatives

Cuisenaire rods are not feasible in larger classes because, obviously, not enough people would be able to see them. Learners can draw/show pictures on the board/screen instead.

This procedure can work well with stories, with dreams or meals or hobbies and skills – just about any subject under the sun!

## Online/virtual variations

Bill Harris (see above) suggests using online resources such as Google Earth rather than Cuisenaire rods. Learners can show pictures to describe their neighbourhoods or to explain how to get from their house to the store or mosque/majid or church, etc.

---

Bilbrough, N. (2011). *Memory Activities for Language Learning*. Cambridge: Cambridge University Press.

Bilbrough, N. (2014). 'Islamabad comes home.' *Humanising Language Teaching*. 16(1), http://old.hltmag.co.uk/feb14/mart01.htm#C7 Accessed 26/02/2021

Stevick, E. (1980). *Teaching Languages: A Way and Ways*. Heinle & Heinle.

For Cuisenaire rods, see https://en.wikipedia.org/wiki/Cuisenaire_rods

# C: Interacting with/from text

Communication in language classrooms does not always have to be *inter*personal, face-to-face speaking as we discussed in 'Why I wrote this book' on page ix. The individual interaction with text, piecing out its meanings, engaging with its context and content is also a form of *intra*personal communication. The learner is communicating with themselves in their own head – and with the images and ideas which the text provokes. Sharing that communication experience with others later returns us to the interpersonal sphere.

## 23 A different point of view

> In this activity, learners use the content and the language
> from a text to reimagine what they have read or heard.

A way of having learners engage fully with the content and the language
of a text and to recreate that is for them to reimagine the scenes/
situations from the points of view of different characters.

1 Tell learners that you are going to tell a story. You may want to use
   a typical storyteller's call-and-response attention-getting technique
   (i.e., when you shout, 'Crick!' they have to shout back, 'Crack!' – a
   technique from Santa Lucia that I learnt from the storytelling of Jan
   Blake) to ensure their listening participation.
2 Start your story (see below for a list of story sources). A lot will
   depend on how you do this. You should try to use your 'best'
   storytelling style by including appropriate (probably exaggerated)
   intonation, sentence and phrase stress, appropriate pausing and
   changes of voice volume, etc. At various stages of the story you
   can use the call-response technique to reawaken their interest and
   participation when/if they seem to be 'flagging' – and to inject pace
   into your telling. You can pause the story and ask the class to predict
   what happens next.
3 When you have finished the story, ask learners to say if they enjoyed
   it and why. You can ask them to say what the 'moral' is or why they
   agree or disagree with the characters, for example.
4 If possible, let learners read the story and ask them to choose any
   'suitcase language' (see 29) they want to take away with them.
5 Learners now think of how they would tell the story from a different
   point of view – i.e., if they were one of the other characters in it.
   How would the story sound then? Give them time to think about
   this and rehearse their telling in their heads.
6 Learners tell the story from the point-of-view of the character
   they have chosen without, if possible, giving away their identity
   immediately. The other learners have to guess who they are.

## Why it works for me

The way that learners have to engage and re-engage with the content, context, etc. of a text makes this a lovely mixture of intrapersonal reflection and purposeful repetition.

## Alternatives

We can choose any number of different stories, of course (see the list below). We need to look for a clear narrative line and where possible, repeated elements (so that learners hear the same linguistic material more than once).

## Online/virtual variations

We can refer learners to stories that we think are appropriate for their level/interest and ask them to read them online following the links we give them. We can give different stories to different learners. Learners can have time to read these stories and become comfortable telling them – preferably without repeating the original word-for-word (i.e., 'in their own words') and they can then tell them to the rest of the group. Alternatively, they can all watch a storytelling video and/or read the same story from a link we send and then they can retell the story from the points of view of different characters and the group can say – in the chatbox – which character they think it is.

---

### Where to find stories

- Harmer, J. and Puchta, H. (2018). *Story-Based Language Teaching*. Helbling.
- Many online newspapers have great real-life stories (see, for example, the Guardian's 'Experience' section).
- Most ELT publishers have graded readers at various levels which can be used in this way.
- *Storytelling With Our Students* by David Heathfield (1980, DELTA publishing) has a collection of useable tales.
- Most coursebooks are full of stories we can tell and have learners re-tell.

# 24   Reassembling poems

> Individual learners are given lines from a poem. In groups, they have to put the lines in the right order without showing them to anyone else.

This is a simple activity, but it demands real concentration and skill. The teacher's participation is crucial as we shall see below.

1   Select a poem you wish to use (see below). The best kind are between nine or ten lines long and have an end-of-line rhyme scheme (limericks, which only have five lines, might nevertheless also be fun). They should be comprehensible for the level you are teaching. Two poems I have used successfully for this activity are *Fire and Ice* by Robert Frost and *Unfortunate Coincidence* by Dorothy Parker. There is a list of poetry resources at the end of **41**.

2   Copy the poem on to a piece of paper and cut it into strips, one for each line. You will start with as many copies of the poem as there will be groups (see 3 below).

3   Now put the class into groups. Each group should have one learner for each line (i.e., groups of six if the poem has six lines).

4   Give each member of each group one of the lines from the poem at random. Tell them that they may not show their lines to each other. They should read their line and practise speaking it in their heads.

5   Ask learners to stand up. Now tell them that they must try and put the lines in the correct order to make the poem. They can read their lines out but (again) they must not show them to each other. Tell them to use only English if they can. It will help if they end up standing in the correct order, so they can 'see' the poem even as they hear and speak it.

6   The activity starts. As it progresses, go round listening to each group and evaluating how well they are doing. You may wish to intervene if they are not making much headway. Sometimes it is necessary to make sure that learners have the correct first line since that starts to unlock the whole thing for them.

7   When a group says they have got the whole poem, listen to check that they have. While they are waiting for other groups to catch up, they should practise speaking it – but quietly!
8   When more than one group has completed the task successfully, have them speak the poem to the rest of the class so that everyone can compare. Now project the poem so that everyone can see it – or give learners a piece of paper with the completed poem on it.
9   Finally, you may want to speak the poem yourself to show how it should sound. Learners can then practise speaking it for themselves and you can help them with pronunciation, pace, pausing and stress.

## Why it works for me

I love poetry of the kind that is appropriate here (clear, reasonably short and engaging). I love the clear and identifiable task that pushes learners to think carefully about what lines mean and how they go together – and this is a communicative group interaction, too.

## Alternatives

We can use this activity as a springboard to poetry performance (see **41**) or poetry learning (see **42**).

## Online/virtual variations

This is perfectly possible to do in an online setting using the 'close your eyes' technique where each learner is given a letter and then all the As, for example, open their eyes to read (and note down) 'their' individual line. We can also use chat/textbox direct messages for this.

**Jigsaw reading**

> Learners read excerpts from a story or article. They then
> talk to others who have read different excerpts. They have
> to discover the complete content of the original.

Like so many activities in early communicative classrooms, *Jigsaw
reading* (and listening – see Geddes and Sturtridge, 1979) is designed
around an information gap. Different learners have different
information (pieces, paragraphs) of a text which, when combined,
allow them to complete the 'jigsaw'. The only way to do this is to
talk about, and share, what they have read. Some of the best kinds of
text for splitting up in this way are stories told from different points
of view, or stories told non-chronologically. Alternatively, texts about
some phenomenon or processes (where different elements go into the
whole text) can be very useful. I have sourced stories and articles from
newspaper sections like the UK Guardian 'Experience' in their Lifestyle
section (for example, a story called 'I caught a falling baby'). See also
the resources listed in **23**.

1 Give learners just one paragraph from a complete story they will
   assemble later. Ideally, this should either be the opening paragraph,
   or something which is not entirely clear – so that learners will want
   to know what it is all about. Tell them to read it carefully. The
   important thing is for everyone to be primed for what they will
   read next.
2 When learners have all read the paragraph, they get into pairs and
   discuss what they think happened or what the article is about. Allow
   them to speculate and discuss this as a whole class, but don't say
   whether their guesses are correct.
3 Divide learners into, say, four groups (A–D). Each group gets a
   paragraph of roughly the same length from the whole text. Tell the
   groups to study their paragraphs carefully. Within the group, they all
   make sure they understand exactly what is going on and what that
   paragraph means.

4  Now make new groups with one learner each from Group A, B, C and D. Learners have to share what they have just read so that they can piece together the sequence of facts and/or events. While they are doing this, go round and help them with things they might have difficulty understanding.

5  Get everyone back together and ask for their versions of the story. Help out with language difficulties and make sure that everyone agrees on the same timeline for the story.

6  You can follow this activity up with procedures detailed in 27 and 29.

**Why it works for me**

The way that a complete picture is slowly assembled, and that this can only be done though purposeful repetition, listening, thought and inter-group participation, ensures that this early communicative activity has stayed around and is included here.

**Alternatives**

The jigsaw concept can be used with listening as well, of course, or with a mixture of video watching and listening. The main aim is to find different jigsaw 'pieces' which learners have to share to make the whole story.

**Online/virtual variations**

In some ways *Jigsaw reading* is as easy online as it is in face-to-face encounters. We can send learners the different texts via email or private messages in the chat/text box or some other communication system. They can form groups in breakout rooms. They can mix speaking and chatbox participation.

Geddes, M. and Sturtridge, G. (1979). *Listening Links*. London: Heinemann Educational Books.

Geddes, M. and Sturtridge, G. (1982). *Reading Links*. London: Heineman Educational Books.

Learners use extracts from something they are going to read (or listen to) to try and predict what that reading will be, using the jigsaw technique.

In 25, the jigsaw technique is used to provoke necessary communication to solve a puzzle. This activity is very similar except that here learners will use it as a way to stimulate their own imaginations. It also prepares them for some reading or listening they are about to do.

In this example at the B2/C1 level, learners get the individual words/ phrases below from an extracted text which they are going to read. It is from the novel *The Ghost* by Robert Harris. It describes the narrator's arrival by ferry, one dark winter's night, at the terminal in Martha's Vineyard, USA, as he is met by a surly deaf taxi driver, who looks at him in the rear view mirror, and is taken to his out-of-season hotel. Wampanoags were the native American tribe who welcomed the Pilgrim fathers and families to America in 1620.

*my suitcase    native Wampanoags    oil paintings*
*rattle of chains    rear view mirror*

1   Divide the class into five groups. Call them A–E. Try to get the groups (if you can) away from each other so they can deliberate without interrupting each other.
2   Give each group one of the words or phrases you have chosen from the text they are going to read. In each group, they should discuss what the word or phrase means and speculate what kind of a text it might appear in. Make sure the learners remember their words/ phrases. You may want to go to the groups to make sure they have understood the correct meaning of what they have been given. They can look things up on the internet.
3   Make new groups of five with one learner from each of the groups A–E. Now ask them to share their words. Tell them they all come from the same text. Their task is to try and work out what the text

is about. While they are doing this, you can go around the groups offering language help and suggestions. You may say things like, 'That's an interesting idea', 'Yes, that's possible, I suppose,' or 'But if it is that, what about this word/phrase?' However, don't tell them if they are right or wrong at this stage.

4  When learners have had time to make their predictions, get them to share their ideas with the rest of the class. Don't tell them who has got it right, but you can ask the class as a whole to guess who is on the right track.

5  Now have learners read the text to see which of their predictions were accurate.

6  Ask them how they feel now, about why they made the predictions they did and what they got wrong and right.

## Why it works for me

I enjoy the fact that a communicative group activity also gives individual learners help in decoding a text later. It is a very 'humane' way of having learners activate their schemata and it ensures they will be especially alert to the language and meaning they encounter.

## Alternatives

There are other ways of having learners discuss their predictions of course: we can create word clouds using the text (see below). Learners can look at all the words and phrases and then discuss their predictions in pairs or groups. We can create the jigsaw effect by using pictures (see **21**).

## Online/virtual variations

We can use the 'close your eyes' technique (see **10**) to give the learners their individual words and phrases online – or use direct messages in the text box – before putting them in their four-person groups in breakout rooms. Of course, we can also use the 'close your eyes' technique in a face-to-face setting too, by projecting the words and phrases on the screen.

**Press conference**

> Learners role play a press conference with characters from
> a passage or story which they have read.

Any fairly dramatic story with multiple characters will be appropriate
here (depending on age and level), but as an example we could tell
learners the true account of a US marine, Zachary Mayo, who fell off
an aircraft carrier into the sea many years ago and was presumed lost
until he was found, amazingly, after two days, floating and delirious in
the middle of the ocean by a Pakistani fisherman (Abdul Aziz) in his
little boat.

1   Introduce learners to the story in the way that is most appropriate
    for the group. You may want to use prediction tasks to prepare
    them and perhaps, after they have experienced the story, ask them
    comprehension questions or extract some language from the story to
    focus on.

2   Lead a discussion with the class. Ask learners what their reactions
    to the story are and talk about that – whether they were fascinated
    or bored will not necessarily matter. The main thing is to make sure
    they are engaged enough with the story to respond to its content.

3   Talk to the learners about the (real-life) characters in the story,
    for example Mayo, his parents, the Marines who went to see the
    parents to announce his disappearance twenty-four hours before he
    was found, the crew members on the aircraft carrier, including the
    captain, and Abdul Aziz. How did it feel from their point of view
    (see 23)? What did they do? What happened next?

4   Put learners in pairs or groups to come up with questions they
    themselves would like to ask the real-life characters and what they
    think their answers might be.

5   Now assign roles to the class. They can be any one of the characters
    (see stage 3 above) or media reporters. A lot will depend on the class.

6   Now hold a press conference with the role players at the front –
    preferably behind a table as in a real press conference. Ask them to
    use their imaginations when they answer!
7   Tell the reporters to make a note of the answers to their questions.
    Tell them that they have to ask a follow-up question when the
    person they are interviewing gives them an answer and make sure
    they do this. You can act the part of the press conference organiser
    for this purpose.
8   Conduct the press conference. Reporters can question who they
    wish. You may want to guide them if the activity slows down.
9   You can run a feedback session where you talk about the activity
    and ask learners for their own evaluation of it. You can add anything
    you think is important in terms of content and language.

## Why it works for me

As with **23**, the press conference makes learners interact with the
text and then with each other. It can be great fun but mimics real
communication in the outside (of class) world. Within those parameters
the six characteristics from 'Why I wrote this book' on page ix are
clearly met.

## Alternatives

Another story of resourceful survival for this activity – depending on
the class – is the 2008 story of 24-year-old Jessica Bruinsma who used
her wits and her sports bra to get herself rescued when she fell onto a
mountain ledge high up in the Bavarian Alps and was facing probable
death until – but you can use a search engine and find out for yourself!

## Online/virtual variations

Since everyone started working and playing so much online, it is not
difficult to replicate this activity using whatever classroom software we
are familiar with/whatever program we are using. This is a role play/
simulation and since many media interviews are conducted online this is
a natural way of doing the activity.

> Learners plan a role play based on a story they have read
> and on the characters in it.

As with the previous activity (see **27**), this role play, described many
years ago by Jane Revell (1979), gets learners to think about what they
will say based on a news story before the role play takes place. We all
too often forget to provide for such pre-activity preparation. Learners
do need to think about what they are going to say and how to say it; it
can become a vital part of the learning process. Any dramatic story with
multiple characters will work with this activity The following example
(based on Harmer, 2004) is pitched at B1 level.

1   Give learners the following words and ask them to put them in a
    sequence to make a newspaper headline: *bites, dispute, dog, fence,
    in, neighbour*. Learners do this in pairs.
2   The class discuss the headline – which should be, 'Neighbour bites
    dog in fence dispute'. They then read an article about William
    Jesperson (47) who bit a dog (which required 4 stitches) belonging
    to his neighbour, Carol Ramsey. She had taken down a fence
    between them and despite promises, had not replaced it because (she
    claimed) she couldn't afford to. It was the dog frightening his child
    and frightening his pet rabbit which proved too much for Jespersen
    and his wife Harmony!
3   Learners read the article (see Harmer, 2004). Then divide the class
    into four groups: William Jesperson, Harmony Jesperson, Carol
    Ramsey and an investigating police office. In their groups, they
    discuss what their characters' justifications are and what they
    will say. The police officer group discusses the kinds of questions
    they might ask and what facts they want to establish. While they
    are doing this, you can go round the groups helping them with
    suggestions and corrective feedback if necessary.
4   Reform the groups so that each one has a police officer, Mr. and
    Mrs. Jespersen and Carol Ramsey. It is the police officer's job to
    ascertain the facts and try to give each person a chance to state their

case. Once again, this is an opportunity to intervene (appropriately) with suggestions.

5 When the 'interviews' have been completed, ask the police officers to compare notes with/in front of the class. This is a good place to give useful feedback to the learners about the task and about the language that was used – and perhaps could have been used!

## Why it works for me

I like the fact that this activity can be serious or – as in our example – somewhat cartoonish, thus allowing learners to have fun. Learners have to think themselves into character and then find the language to express that.

## Alternatives

Instead of group work, we can have learners work in pairs where one learner is the police officer and the other is one of the other three characters. Our learner grouping will be different, of course. When the interviews are over, the police officers can compare their conclusions and what they have been told with the rest of the class.

Any news story can be used in this way, provided that it has the potential to engage our learners. We can also invent our own scenarios or give learners only a newspaper headline and have them invent a story to go with it and then proceed with the activity from there.

## Online/virtual variations

It would be just as easy, online, to use a video news clip – rather than a written article – as the story for this activity. We can share it or send learners to an internet link.

If we don't want to spend too much time organising groups into breakout rooms, we can use the whole class and the chat/text box to discuss the original story and what the characters might say. Then we can put learners in pairs (see Alternatives above). Using any kind of breakout grouping is helped if we decide before the lesson how to assign the learners.

Harmer, J. (2004). *Just Right Student's Book Intermediate*. Marshall Cavendish.

Revell, J. (1979). *Teaching Techniques for Communicative English*. Macmillan Publishers, republished Harper Collins Publishers (2013).

> Learners choose the words they would most like to 'put
> in their suitcase' and then explain why and how they will
> use them. In groups, they use these words to create their
> own text.

This all started for me when I came up with (or perhaps inadvertently
'borrowed') the idea of 'desert island words' to have learners try and
engage with words in lists at the end of units in books. Such wordlists
usually just sit there with no one paying them any attention, but if we
ask learners to choose which five words they would take to a desert
island and why, they have to think about the words and talk about them.

My activity bears a strong similarity, I discovered, to an activity which
originates, I believe, from Sheelagh Deller's concept of 'Fridge, dustbin,
suitcase,' where learners decide whether they want to keep new words
for later use, throw them away because they don't want them, or put
them in their suitcase. I have focused on the third of these. The 'suitcase'
metaphor encourages learners to make individual choices about the
language they, individually, wish to prioritise in their learning.

1   After learners have read a text, watched a video or listened to an
    audio track, ask them to do it again. This time, however, they have to
    choose the three words or phrases in the text that they would most
    like to 'put in their suitcase and take home with them'. Emphasise
    that they are doing this because it is they, not the materials or the
    teacher, who can determine how and what they wish to learn. This
    may be somewhat fanciful given the pressures of tests and exams, for
    example, but the concept of the suitcase sends a powerful message
    to them about autonomy and self-empowerment. Tell learners that
    they have to be able to justify their reasons. Why do they like their
    choices? Why do they think they might be useful?
2   Learners now take their choices and research them online (they can
    use a search engine or access an online dictionary, for example).

They should think of examples of how they can use them and come up with sentences/contexts for that purpose.

3 Now group learners together and ask them to share their choices – and give examples of how they can use them.

4 The group now decides on the four words or phrases the whole group most wants to put in their metaphorical group suitcase. They will have to negotiate with each other.

5 The groups share their words and phrases and give examples. Make adjustments, if/where necessary.

## Why it works for me

This activity provokes intrapersonal interaction between the learners' language processing and the texts they are engaged with. It also, crucially, is a potent reminder that they, as learners, are at the top of the teaching and learning pyramid. By 'humanising' words and phrases and then discussing them with others it expresses what learning is all about.

## Alternatives

We could have some fun by assigning individual learners different numbers, randomly. They then have to choose say, the third, fourth, seventh, etc. word in each sentence (or in some selected sentences). They then get into groups as before.

Learners could draw the words or phrases they have chosen, and other learners have to try to guess what they are (see also 10). They could say which three words or phrases they would take to a desert island and why.

## Online/virtual variations

There is no reason for not using this activity in an online setting. Learners can hear a story (we can tell it, or they can watch a video or listen to an audio) and then read it – this can happen through screenshare, or we can link them to the text. They then choose their suitcase language individually before we put them in breakout groups where they share their words, make their choices, and then explain them to the whole group.

# D: Making decisions

Activities in this section ask learners –
in groups – to talk to each other so
that they can decide on what to do, on
what is true, on what is important, etc.
Provoking learners to reach a decision
and arrive at a conclusion is a way
of ensuring communication between
individuals, a communication that is
bound to engender the kind of deep
processing that I talked about in 'Why
I wrote this book' on page ix. And where
decisions have to be reiterated, defended
and negotiated, a virtuous circle of
effective classroom communication
is created.

Learners decide what criteria they wish to use to judge a photographic prize. They then use their criteria to choose the winner from one of, say, four photos. They give reasons for their choices.

We all consume images all the time, whether on our phones, in the media or in galleries. But how good are we at interpreting what we are looking at? This activity works well with teenagers and upwards. In my experience, the higher the level, the better the conversation.

1   Start by having a discussion with learners about when/if they look at photographs. This is a good opportunity to elicit key concepts for the forthcoming activity – black and white photography, digital photography, selfies, telescopic photography. Decide how detailed you want to be here depending on the level of the learners. Ask them if there are any famous photographs they can remember. You could show them a photograph which you think is especially memorable.

2   Now that learners have started to consider photographs, tell them that they are going to be judges for an international historical photograph choice – they will choose a photograph to be included in a photography exhibition. The category is 'People in black and white'. They have to decide on four categories which they will use to reach their decision. Discuss these categories with the whole group or put students in groups with an uneven number (so that a majority decision can be reached).

3   If you have not formed the groups yet, do it now. Give each group four photographs; I have used (a) *Migrant Mother* by Dorothea Lange, (b) *Elizabeth Eckford and Hazel Bryan* by William Counts, (c) *Men on a Rooftop* by René Burri and (d) *Burst of Joy* by Slava (Sal) Vader (see Harmer and Lethaby, 2005). Of course, any, perhaps more modern, photos can be used.

4   Tell learners to look at the pictures in silence for a few moments and to consider which of the four photos they would choose based

on the four categories they decided on in stage 2 (above). Now they have to discuss which photograph the group will pick as the one that best answers those four categories.

5   When the groups have made their choices, ask each to share not only their photograph, but more importantly, the reason for their choice, based on the four categories in stage 2.

6   If more than one photo is chosen, let learners vote, as individuals, for which photo they would like to win.

## Why it works for me

I like this activity because learners have something real to discuss (with all the activity benefits discussed in 'Why I wrote this book' on page ix). Everyone can have a valid and thoughtful opinion and the decision (with classroom limitations) matters.

## Alternatives

We can have a class photography competition where all learners take and then submit a photo on a particular theme and post it online for everyone to see. We have a quick vote about which photos are the best (learners can't vote for their own pictures) and choose the highest scoring photographs.

There is any number of alternatives to photographs. It could be the best drawing, painting, sculpture, building or poem, for example. Learners could themselves write poems, compositions, do drawings, or some other creative activity. This will give everyone a really personal stake in the outcome!

## Online/virtual variations

We can use a judicious mix of the chat/text box, plenary sessions, breakout/side rooms when doing this activity online. We can ask learners to discuss their suggestions all together – with suggestions in the chatbox. We can share our screen so that they see the photos and give them time to look at what they see, making notes as they do. They can then get into groups and decide on which photo they will choose before coming back to the main group.

Harmer, J. and Lethaby, C. (2005). *Just Right Student's Book Upper Intermediate*. Marshall Cavendish.

Learners encounter a problem situation which provides a dilemma about how people should react. They have to decide how to resolve the dilemma before enacting it for the rest of the class.

What is the best way out of a difficult situation? Which of many courses of action are the best? We all face such dilemmas, big and small, in our daily lives. We can introduce dilemmas into our classrooms, too, so that learners have to agree on how to resolve them. The example below (at the B2 level) is one such possibility.

1   The learners listen to the audio of a conversation from the reference below between a primary headteacher and two boys, Joe and Malcolm. Once Ms Griffiths (the headteacher) has prised the story out of them, she sums everything up:
    *TEACHER So let me get this straight. Malcolm hurt your friend by pulling the chair out from under him when he was about to sit down and that made you angry. You stood up for your friend. But then he provoked you some more and that made you even madder and that's when you hit him. Is that right, Joe?*
    *JOE Yes, Ms. Griffiths.*
    *TEACHER Alright then. Well, I'm glad we've got that straight. The question is what are we going to do about it?*
2   Now ask what the headteacher should do with the boys. Should she (a) make the boys decide what to do next, (b) make the boys shake hands, (c) praise Joe, (d) punish Joe, (e) punish Malcom, (f) do something else? Learners get together in groups of three, five or seven to decide what Miss Griffiths should do. The groups now compare their decisions and, perhaps, the class votes on the best one.
3   Now ask learners to role play the scene (see 27 and 28) using their own language, and, hopefully, language which they picked up from the conversation they have heard. They can do this first in groups and then perform for the rest of the class.

## Why it works for me

The communicative interaction necessary for choosing the right solution satisfies the six conditions discussed in 'Why I wrote this book' (see page ix) especially because of the interaction within the group and the uses to which language is being put – and repeated.

## Alternatives

You can present the learners with dilemmas by telling the stories yourself. Put learners in groups of three and give each member of the group a role-card. The roles for our example are the headteacher, Malcolm or Joe. Here is Malcolm's card – not to be shown to the others.

> *You have been sent to see the headteacher because you were in a fight with another student, Joe, who hit you first. You will say it was his fault. What you don't really want to say (you may have to) is that you hurt Joe's friend by pulling the chair from under him and then you taunted Joe about it (you made faces at him and you taunted his friend).*

You can use many other dilemmas: what should you do if you caught a student cheating, but their home situation was really difficult? What should someone do if they find a lot of cash; hand it in or keep it? What should you do if you see a mother smacking a child in the supermarket?

## Online/virtual variations

We can share an audio of the conversation online (or direct learners to a link to the audio) and then put them in breakout/separate rooms to discuss the situation before everyone gives their opinion. We can screenshare a dilemma scenario – or tell people about it. Learners can use the chat/textbox for this too.

--------------------------------------------------------------------------------

Harmer, J. and Revell, J. (2017). *Jetstream Upper-intermediate*. Helbling.

> Learners decide – individually and then in groups – which national or international figures or activities they will put on a new issue of stamps.

I first came across this activity some time ago in Peter Moor and Sarah Cunningham's coursebook series *Cutting Edge* (Moor and Cunningham, 1998). Today, even in a world of electronic and digital communication, currencies and stamps are still issued which commemorate people, places and events.

1 Have a discussion with the class about whether they ever buy stamps anymore. Ask learners if they receive letters or parcels with stamps on them. It is a good idea to have examples on hand which show what stamps look like and have looked like – especially those which show a person on them.

2 Tell learners to think about world figures or people from their own countries or communities, people they admire and think they made a great contribution through their lives and actions. They should do this individually. Tell learners to make notes about why they might be a suitable figure to put on the country's stamps. This is an important stage in the activity because it gives learners thinking time – a vital element if they are to have the confidence to express themselves in the foreign language. We sometimes forget to give them such time!

3 Now put learners in pairs or groups. They talk about who they have chosen and why. They should do this by going round the group one by one. The learners make a note of the names. When they have all stated their choice, the group votes on who, as a group, they are going to choose. If there is a tie, or if some people are still unhappy, they restate their arguments – using different words to say them – until the group finally agrees on their choice. While learners are discussing in this way, circulate, offering help and support with language and prompting people to speak where the conversations falter.

4   Now the groups share their choices with the class.
5   When all the choices have been stated, the class votes on who should be put on the country's/world's stamps! Keep a tally of how many votes are cast.
6   Now offer people who voted for the least successful person a last chance to state their case. As with all stages, keep a record (on paper, on a device or in your head) of what was said.
7   The class votes again. Now you have a consensus.
8   Using what you have noted down, talk about the good arguments you heard, suggest ways of saying things better and maybe draw learners' attention to language problems which have occurred.

## Why it works for me

This activity has a CLIL feel (see 38) where, as in the previous two examples, content really matters. It allows often quite heated (but safe) debate and thus really focuses learners' minds on effective communicative strategies and language use.

## Alternatives

Another possibility which may, in fact, provoke more and wider discussion is choosing who to make a statue of. Statues and memorials have become a sensitive issue – in terms of historical context, gender representation, etc. in recent years. Deciding who to install statues of and where to put them has great potential as an effective communicative activity. We can also talk about which figures we would like to see on our country's printed currency (for however long we continue to use paper money!), or give a national medal to or nominate as 'person of the year'. This topic has caused controversy in many countries, in particular, the absence of women and other groups.

## Online/virtual variations

This activity (and the statues alternative) will work well in an online environment if we put groups in breakout rooms to make their decisions before coming to a class consensus.

Moor, P. and Cunningham, S. (1998). *Cutting Edge Intermediate*. Longman.

Learners decide what they should put in a time capsule for the future. They can role play what people say when it is opened.

For the life of me, I can't remember where I first came across the idea of using the concept of a time capsule for decision-making, but it makes absolute sense! People have wanted to preserve history forever, of course – documents, paintings, statues, sacred relics, etc. Among the earliest examples of deliberate planning are from the 18th century where collections of letters and objects were hidden in statues or the foundations of buildings. There have been four time capsules sent to space in case extraterrestrial beings come across them. True, historians are on the whole sceptical of the idea, seeing the decontextualised unpacking of objects at some time in the future as being unhelpful for future investigators. Nevertheless, many people are fascinated by the concept.

1   Ask learners if they are familiar with the idea of a time capsule. Explain that people put things/recordings in a container and bury it in a secret location to be opened, say, 100 years later (see above).

2   Ask learners how they would describe life today. What things would they show/tell a visitor from another planet to explain what life is like? Various suggestions might be: photographs, videos, letters, objects, internet content, toys, speeches, letters/emails/ messages, etc. Learners can discuss this in pairs or small groups – or as the whole class.

3   Tell learners to select ten objects to put in an indestructible container no bigger than a document box. They should do this individually first, and give them a few minutes to think about this. They can write down their suggestions and consider their reasons.

4   Learners now discuss their choices in pairs. You can prepare these discussions with useful enabling language such as, 'I think we should definitely include X.' 'Surely Y is more important?' 'The most

obvious thing to include is Z.' Pairs should come to agreement on about ten items. This will involve negotiation on both sides.

5 Now combine pairs into small groups and the negotiation process starts again.

6 Depending on the size of the class, you can now combine two groups, and then four groups, etc.

7 Finally, have the whole class discuss what should go into the time capsule until you have, hopefully, a class consensus. Comment (with supportive feedback) on what you have heard and how it was said.

## Why it works for me

I like the reflective nature of this activity. Who are we? What represents our way of living best? That is surely something worth discussing and, as with content-based teaching of various kinds (CLIL, ESP, etc.), it takes sometimes very language-focused classrooms out into areas of motivating general interest.

## Alternatives

We can use some similar ranking tasks such as ten things people would take to survive on a desert island; the relative levels of pay in different professions in an ideal world (should a primary teacher earn more than a university teacher, for example?); or the desirable qualities for certain occupations – president, gardener, nurse, etc. (See 37.)

## Online/virtual variations

We can ask learners to research the topic of 'time capsule'. What has gone into past time capsules? They share what they find out with the group either orally, or in the chat box.

After facilitating discussion with the whole online group, the process can be repeated using breakout rooms. Learners can show items they want to include.

When a decision has been made, learners can make short videos explaining their choices and post them to an intranet system or a public site (though we must keep safeguarding issues in mind).

Learners design and (if possible) produce a T-shirt
representing their country, club or school, etc.

I watched Mark Andrews teach a demonstration class during a
conference in Poland. To the obvious delight of the learners, he wove
a narrative around the different labelling on beer bottles, from both
English-speaking and non-English-speaking countries. His T-shirt
activity (which I have adapted for inclusion in this collection) is based
on the same kind of idea (see also **30–34**).

1 Ask learners to think about the different things that go on T-shirts
  which are illustrated in some way (pictures, designs, names, images,
  logos, etc.). What are their favourite T-shirts? They should describe
  them or bring photographs. Why do they like them? Because of
  memories associated with the T-shirt? Because of how they look?

2 After learners show/talk about their T-shirts, tell them that they are
  going to plan a T-shirt to reflect their country (or country in which
  they are studying). What should go on it? They can choose up to
  six images/things to represent, e.g., facts, qualities, foods, national
  characteristics or places in their country.

3 Learners now work on their own to think about how to represent
  their country. If you see one of them looking blank, you can prompt
  with questions about famous buildings and places – or geographical
  features or anything else.

4 Now put learners in pairs and ask them to share their ideas and try
  to agree on up to six things to go on the T-shirt. You can give them
  enabling language such as, 'We could put/include …' 'Perhaps we
  could …' 'X might look better/make a stronger impact,' etc.

5 Combine the pairs into groups and have them try and see if between
  them they can come up with a T-shirt that is to their satisfaction.
  Give them time to discuss this. Point out that they must give
  coherent reasons for not agreeing that something should be included.
  Learners should be prepared to argue enthusiastically for what

they wish to include. While they are doing this, you can go round the groups offering supportive feedback where appropriate. You may want to prompt them to say more about why they believe the opinions which they are expressing. The groups draw their designs.

6   When the activity is finished, the groups present their T-shirts to the rest of the class. They can use the board to show what they mean. You can gently intervene to help them clarify things.

7   The class now votes on the best T-shirt design. They can vote for their own design, but *only* if they genuinely believe it is the best one.

8   Learners can work on actually creating the winning T-shirt either through drawing, or digital photoshopping.

## Why it works for me

The personal nature of the topic, and the content it deals with, should ensure cognitive – but also emotional – connection. Very much a group interaction, *T-shirt* has all the aspects of an effective communicative activity.

## Alternatives

For individual learners, we can ask them to say what *they* would like on the front and back of their own T-shirt words, images, or whatever. They should explain why they have made their choices. Of course, this loses some of the effectiveness of a communicative activity. Apart from countries, learners can talk about their town, their football club, their school, their language, etc. A lot will depend on the composition of the class you are teaching.

## Online/virtual variations

We can have learners do this as an individual task, maybe before the lesson starts. We can have the same discussion as in stages 1 and 2 and then set the task. Next lesson they can show their designs and explain them using screen share or showing a drawing or a picture. The class votes using the symbols which the software provides.

# The party  35

Learners decide on a party – when, where, how, what with, etc. – to celebrate an event.

Some years ago, together with some other participants in a seminar I was speaking at, I observed a lesson in Beijing, China. There were nearly sixty teenagers in the group, studying at an intermediate level B2. They sat, tightly packed, at round tables in groups of four. After doing some work on items of language, each table (group of four) had to organise an imaginary celebratory party. The observers were asked to judge the best party plan. It was, to this day, one of the best lessons I have observed: beautifully managed, carefully staged and with the complete involvement of the teenagers. There could be many reasons for this, but one of them was the appropriacy, for those groups, of the task itself.

1   Tell learners they are going to be planning a party – a celebration. You may want to suggest what they will be celebrating. It could be the end of the year, someone's birthday, a special date in the calendar, etc. You can make it as 'fantastical' as you wish. It could be a party on a boat, on a space station(!) or anywhere else you and the learners choose. Your choice will depend on the age and the level of the students.
2   Ask learners to spend a few minutes, individually, thinking about what kind of a party it is going to be. They should make notes of their ideas. They will use these ideas for the next stages.
3   Put learners into groups of four or five (an uneven number is often better when decisions have to be reached). Tell them to share their ideas – and give them a time limit for this. Each member of the group says what they have thought of, and the other members of the group ask questions about their ideas.
4   Tell learners to use all the ideas to come to a decision on what kind of party their group wants to have. They should make individual notes on their decisions. While they are doing this you can go round the groups prompting and suggesting – and helping out with language difficulties where necessary.

73

5 When the activity is over, ask each member of the group to have a separate number from 1–5 (if they are in groups of five). Now choose a number and point to a group: the learner who has that number has to describe their party. I borrowed this 'numbered heads' ideas from William Littlewood (2004). It was his way of trying to ensure that all learners would be equally involved because they didn't know who was going to be picked.

6 When all the groups have described their plans, they can vote for the best party – one vote for their own party and one for another group's effort.

## Why it works for me

This activity works because all learners (people) can relate to it, because it is simple to explain, and because it has a clear outcome – the party plan itself. As we discussed in 'Why I wrote this book', purposeful repetition and group interaction are two important characteristics of effective communicative activities and they are both in evidence here.

## Alternatives

Learners could plan for/organise a flashmob (where people turn up unannounced in a public place unexpectedly and perform a song or a dance, etc.), a protest activity, a holiday or a trip. Just about any group activity will do!

## Online/virtual variations

Ideally, put learners in groups into breakout rooms and set a time limit for them to plan a party. While they are doing this you can visit the rooms to make sure the learners are on task, and to help them with suggestions, etc. If breakout rooms are not an option for any reason, you can have the whole group plan a class party and their suggestions can be made both to camera and also in the chat/textbox.

Littlewood, W. (2004). 'Structuring classroom interaction for task-based learning.' Paper presented at the 38th annual IATEFL conference.

Individual learners are given a different picture. In small groups, they have to share the contents of their picture without showing it to anyone else. They have to decide what links the different pictures.

This is similar to our story reconstruction activity (**21**) and shares the same underlying 'information gap' protocols as activities such as *Jigsaw reading* (see **25**) and others (see **18**). Learners must find a common link between four apparently unrelated items.

1 Put learners into groups, one for each of the pictures you are going to show them.

2 Give each group a (different) photograph. In the example from the reference below, the photographs show (a) The President of the United States (or any other country!), (b) a surfer riding a large wave, (c) a nuclear power station, (d) an aircraft carrier, (e) a large hydroelectric dam. It is important that the pictures do all share a theme but, depending on the group, you do not want to make it as obvious as, say, five different forms of transport, because the resulting conversation would be very short!

3 Each group is told to look at the picture they have been given. They should discuss what it shows (you can support them with language such as: 'It seems to be …' 'It's a big picture of …' 'It might suggest …') and tell each other anything they know or think about what they are seeing.

4 Take the pictures back from the groups.

5 Now reform the groups so that the new groups all have one learner from group A, one learner from Group B, one learner from group C, etc.

6 Tell the learners to talk to each other about the pictures they saw in their original group. They can tell the others about the discussions they had there.

7   We now tell the learners that they must discuss what possible connection there is between the photographs they have each looked at. What common theme is represented in all of the pictures? Set a time limit for this (you may want to put the time into your phone to make the activity more 'exact'). Tell them that they can come up with more than one possible connection if they want. While they are doing this you can go round the class helping out with language difficulties and making sure that the learners are on task.

8   When the activity has finished, discuss what the groups have decided with the whole class. Don't agree or disagree with their suggestions at this point, but rather ask the class to decide which choice is the most convincing (the theme that was intended, incidentally, is 'power' – which all the pictures represent different aspects of).

**Why it works for me**

This activity allows some learners to have one of those 'lightbulb' moments. In pursuit of that possibility, language becomes enabling and instinctive. I believe this is part of the processing that leads to automaticity.

**Alternatives**

Each student gets a different short poem. They study it and then talk to each other to find/invent connections. How many poems are about love? How many are difficult to understand? How many are loved by their reader? How many criticise war? This is an ideal *Everybody up* activity (see **1**). See also activities **41** and **42**. You could also have learners write cryptic quiz clues – where the answers to, say, four different questions when combined give you the answer to the main question you asked.

**Online/virtual variations**

*What's the link?* is entirely appropriate for use online. We can either show learners in different breakout rooms different photographs, objects or words/phrases and then re-combine them into different groups or we can use the 'close your eyes' technique (see activity **10**).

Harmer, J., Wilson, K., Lethaby, C. and Acevedo, A. (2009). *Just Right Advanced*. Cengage Heinle.

Learners have to decide who, from a number of people, will be the last survivor of a life-threatening situation or event.

This game has been around for as long as anyone can remember, and it goes like this: a group of people argue why they should survive some cataclysmic event when all others perish. The rest of the class decides who it will be. The version we are going to describe here is probably the best-known of all its versions, the *Balloon debate*.

1 Give learners a list of occupations, for example: airline pilot, artist, doctor, farmer, medical researcher, musician/composer, plumber, scientist, software engineer, teacher, truck driver, etc.

2 Put learners in groups. In a set time limit (seven minutes, perhaps) they have to list what benefits each of these occupations brings to society. The purpose of this stage is to give learners some thinking time so that they have something to say – and an idea of how to say it.

3 Explain the 'last survivor' scenario. Say that a number of people with different professions are in the basket of a hot air balloon. The only problem is that the balloon has a tear and it is losing air. Someone will have to jump out to lighten the load. Explain that the people in the basket will each have to say why they should be the one to survive.

4 Select the learners who will be in the balloon basket and allocate them a different profession. Depending on how many learners you have in the class you can limit the number of professions you have in the basket. Give them some time to marshal their thoughts. They can make notes about what they are going to say. While they are doing this, you can take a vote with the others to say who they think – before hearing the arguments – should survive and why. They can think of questions they would like to ask each of the people in that basket!

5 Set up the front of the classroom as the 'balloon basket'. The occupants of the basket can sit in a semi-circle facing the class.

6 Each participant explains – in a maximum of three minutes per person – why they should be the one to survive the crisis and therefore not have to jump.

7 The rest of the class who are listening can now ask questions to the basket occupants and say what they think about what they have heard.

8 When everyone 'in the basket' has spoken, the class votes on who should be allowed to survive. Learners may only vote for one person. Tell them they should base their decision on how well the different cases were argued.

9 The person who got the smallest number of votes has to leave the basket. They join the rest of the class.

10 The process is repeated. Each time one person has to leave until finally there is a winner.

## Why it works for me

*The last survivor* works because it is often great fun! Learners have to really listen in order to cast their vote. In the preparation stage they have to focus on the best language to use in their groups. To my mind it satisfies the six characteristics detailed in 'Why I wrote this Book' on page ix.

## Alternatives

If you don't like doomsday scenarios(!), learners can vote on 'the most important occupation' to include in a government or they can choose a well-known celebrity and argue why they should win the 'personality of the year' competition – and so on.

## Online/virtual variations

Using breakout rooms, we can have learners do their group work as before. While the chosen speakers are preparing their arguments, we and the rest of the group can talk about which profession we think might survive. Learners can use the online platform's emojis or chat/text box to vote.

# E: Presenting and performing things

Activities in this section all ask learners to do something – to perform something, tell something, or video something, for example. They focus learners on the language they have encountered and/or will use, whilst at the same time making the manner of communication a focus. Some learners, individually, are not keen on performing in front of others. That is why these activities are mostly focused on group presentation, where attention on the individual is subsumed into the behaviour of the group as a collective of collaborating individuals.

> Learners research facts about animals in groups in order
> to tell their classmates which of a random pair they would
> rather be.

In this activity we combine language research with critical thinking on a topic that learners aged around eight to twelve and at A2 level may find very agreeable.

Sugata Mitra (2013) is one of many people to suggest that children can learn without being 'fed' facts if we simply ask them the right questions and give them the tools to research their answers collaboratively (rather than doing so individually). Mitra's argument suggested the arrival of the online world made this possible.

*I'd rather* fits into the thinking behind CLIL (Content and Language Integrated Learning) which suggests that language should be at the service of (and enable learners to talk about) content rather than the other way round (see, for example, Coyle, Hood and Marsh, 2009).

1 Write the names of animals, birds, insects and fishes on separate pieces of paper. Fold the pieces of paper so that the names are not visible and put all the pieces of paper in a hat, bag or bowl (see also 8).
2 Divide the class into groups of five. A representative from each group comes and chooses two pieces of paper (= two animals, etc.).
3 The groups gather round a tablet or a screen hooked up to the internet or intranet. If these are not available, learners can access books in the school library and bring them back to the group.
4 Ask learners, in their groups, to research the two animals they have chosen, for example, an elephant and a scorpion, a whale and a mouse, a tiger and a lion. Learners find out at least five things about each animal – where they live, how long they live, what they do, who wants to kill them, etc. They discuss their information.
5 The learners assemble the facts they have discovered about both animals to prepare to say why they would rather be animal A than animal B. Tell them to plan to present their findings to the class.

6   Each group presents their findings to the class. They might say, for
    example, that they would rather be an ant than an elephant because
    people do not usually try to kill them and there is always plenty of
    food for them. Elephants don't have enough food in many places
    and people want to kill them for their tusks. Each member of the
    group has to contribute and give some of the reasons they have
    decided on. You can, at the end of the lesson ask learners to say
    which animal, really, they would most like to be and why!

## Why it works for me

I like the playful and thought-provoking processes that learners go
through for this deceptively simple activity. The purposeful repetition
and interactions are an added bonus.

## Alternatives

There are many different ways of using (and topics for) this research and
presentation activity. With older learners, we could write world cities
on the pieces of paper. The groups then have to research the cities and
present to the group about which of their pairs they would rather live
in and why. At higher levels/ages, learners could concentrate on musical
instruments, extreme sport challenges, climate change solutions, etc.

## Online/virtual variations

We can send individual learners an email/message with an animal for
them to research online (each student gets a different animal). You can
then pair up any two learners to share their two animals and then each
can make sentences to the whole group about why they would rather be
'their' animal than the other one.

Coyle, D., Hood, P. and Marsh, D. (2009). *Content and Language Integrated Learning.*
Cambridge: Cambridge University Press.

Mitra, S. (2013). https://www.youtube.com/watch?v=y3jYVe1RGaU
Accessed: July 29, 2019

## 39 Revision charades

> Learners play a popular party game but with a revision twist. Individuals act out recently learnt or encountered sentences while members of their team try to guess the sentence with language-based questions.

Originating (we think) in 18th century France, *Charades* had evolved by the mid-19th century into the 'acted out' version of today's party game. Our version mixes this with language-based revision.

1   Divide the class into two teams. In each team, ask the learners to come up with sentences (no longer than 10–12 words) from last week's classes (grammar sentences, sentences from texts, etc.). They should write each one on a different strip of paper.

2   Tell learners that they will each be given their own individual sentence (by the other team) and that after a few seconds thinking about it (and about its grammar), they will have to act it out and answer questions about it. The other learners in their team can then ask them *yes/no* questions about the sentence's language and syntax, e.g., 'Is the first word a definite article?' 'Are there any prepositions in the sentence?' 'Is the third word a verb?' 'Is the sentence in the past?' or 'If there are adjectives, are they positive or negative?' etc.

3   Team A selects one of the sentences they have written down and hands it over to a player in team B. That player has 20–30 seconds to think about how they are going to mime it. Now they act it out to their team (B) who try and guess what is going on. Each learner can ask a question about the sentence (see 2 above).

4   The team now has a second round of questions – and if necessary, a third. Keep a record of how many rounds it takes for the sentence to be guessed correctly.

5   Now team B gives someone from team A one of the sentences they (team B) have written. Team A now goes through the same sequence described in stage 3. Again, keep a record of how many rounds it takes for the sentence to be guessed correctly.

6   When all the pieces of paper have been used – or earlier if the game has lost its momentum – the activity finishes. But if you do finish the activity 'early', you must be absolutely sure that each team has had the same number of 'turns'. With any game, learners often get highly incensed if they perceive unfairness, even where the game itself is fairly light-hearted.

7   Now count up all the scores and the team with the lowest scores (i.e., who had the least total rounds to get the sentences right) is the winner. All the sentences can be projected, and you can draw attention to salient language features.

## Why it works for me

This activity is highly motivating, and it is great fun. It involves processing for meaning and has the learners interact with language and the context(s) that language occurs in. It promotes group cohesion – especially among members of the same team. But at the same time, it acts as a language-focused revision procedure!

## Alternatives

Any simple mime activity which involves performing and guessing works really well. For example, learners can act out something that happened to them and the other learners have to guess the story. They can mime any simple activity – climbing a mountain, playing a violin, cooking a meal, etc. for their classmates. Rather than acting out a sentence or phrase, we can have learners create and then speak a monologue or a dialogue which suggests the sentence or phrase they have been given.

## Online/virtual variations

*Revision charades*, especially, works well online since individual learners can ask their questions one-by-one – to camera or using the chat/textbox. The mix of the two (speaking to camera, and chat box interactions) is remarkably effective. The problem comes with the camera: how 'wide-angle' is it? In other words, can we see the gestures and movements that this activity demands? If not, we can use the monologue/dialogue equivalent (see above).

# 40 Playscript

Learners, in pairs or groups, work on a scene from a play or movie. They rehearse it and then perform it for their colleagues who comment on the performance.

Some years ago, I went to a superbly well-acted performance of Eugene O'Neill's play *Long Day's Journey into Night* in a London theatre. I was struck by the often-discussed fact that the actors repeated the same exact lines every evening and yet they sounded freshly spoken and moving to me that night. And they were probably different each night depending on their mood and the audience in the hall. This is surely the 'resignification' that Claire Kramsch talks about (see page ix) on a grand scale. Which is why some teachers have embraced drama as a perfect language learning/practising activity (see also **44**).

1   Give learners a playscript to read. The ideal length of the script will depend on time available and learners' language level, age, etc. In general, 'small is beautiful'. There are suggestions for resourcing scripts below.

2   Talk about the script with the class. Is it funny? Serious? Enjoyable? With younger learners, help them engage with the scene by asking questions like, 'Do you like the characters?' 'What do they look like, do you think?' You can also tell the class something about the play(script) which might help them imagine the scene visually and 'hear' the words in their heads.

3   Clear up any misunderstanding of words and phrases in the scene. Ask learners how they think lines should be spoken. Loud or soft? High voices, low voices, fast or slow? Have them mark their scripts to help them remember this and get them to say the lines that way. Try not to make it look as if there is a 'right' way to say the lines. You want learners to explore possibilities for themselves, with your guidance.

4   In pairs (or trios or groups, depending on the number of characters in the scene), learners practise speaking the script to get them familiar with saying the lines.

5  Now make groups with the same number as the characters and perhaps one more person to act as 'director'. First, ask learners to decide who will take which parts and who will be the director. Now they start to rehearse again, and the director leads the discussion and gives guidance. They discuss how they will perform to the rest of the class.

6  Learners perform their versions to the class. Ask for comments from the class and offer your own feedback.

## Why it works for me

We discussed 'resignification' above – and everything that says about purposeful repetition. Learners also give attention to suprasegmental pronunciation issues (such as intonation, stress, pausing, etc.), and they process the script and talk about it, together.

## Alternatives

We can get learners to write their own scenes, of course and, after we have helped them to check their English, the procedure can work as before. In **44,** we will discuss how this can lead on to a longer filming sequence.

## Online/virtual variations

When using online classroom platforms, we can choose scripts that would work as radio plays. We can all talk about the scene and different ways of speaking the lines before learners go into their breakout groups. They then come back and perform. We will have to help learners to come to terms with the fact that quick interruptions, etc. (a normal part of face to face acting) won't work here; they will have to be aware of pausing after every speaker and build that into their performances. We can add an extra element by asking them to include sound effects like Foley artists do for radio and film.

---

### Where to find playscripts

- http://www.aaronshep.com/rt/ has playscript resources for children.
- https://www.theatrefolk.com/blog/playwriting-performance-esl-classroom/ gives advice and playscripts for ESL learners.
- Wilson, K. and Case, D. (1979) *Off Stage*. Macmillan – has a collection English teaching scripts.
- Some teachers have used writers like Samuel Beckett and Harold Pinter for acting out! Simple words, short speeches, but complex meanings.

## 41

**Poetry enactment**

In this activity, groups are given the responsibility of performing a poem for the class after a period of preparation – with only very minimal teacher help.

I first encountered this activity, as a participant, in a workshop being run by Alan Pulverness and Sarah Mount. They, in their turn, had encountered it in a workshop by Alan Maley. It is probably my personal favourite of all the activities in this book. I have organised it in many different locations around the world with learners as well as teachers. It has never failed. What never ceases to amaze me is the creativity that people bring to the task, whatever their age.

1 Organise learners into groups of five to seven.
2 Give each learner a copy of a poem. It should not be too long and it should be appropriately transparent. In other words, the meaning should not be hidden too much by poetic technique. Ideally, it should clearly express identifiable situations and emotions. There are suggestions for resourcing poems below.
3 Tell groups that in 25 minutes they will have to perform the poem for the rest of the class, any way they want. For example, they can get one member to speak the poem and the others to interpret, act or repeat lines; they can do it in chorus; they could do it one word per participant at a time; they can sing it, dance it, draw it – whatever comes to mind. The only stipulations are that (a) the poem must be spoken/sung somehow and (b) every single member of the group must play an observable part in the performance.
4 Learners work in their groups. Between them they have to understand the poem using whatever means they have to hand (each other, dictionaries, you). Where possible, groups can leave the classroom for their preparation – they can go to the corridor, the library, the computer room or wherever (provided, obviously that these rooms are not being used by other people!). While they are doing this, circulate to make sure they are on task.

5 When the time is up, the groups perform their poem to the class. Your role is to be as encouraging and positive as possible and to make sure that each group is listened to/watched with attention.

6 When each group has performed, clear up any misunderstandings about language. Ask learners to comment on and/or ask questions about the poems, the performances and the activity itself.

## Why it works for me

By demanding a profound understanding of meaning which a whole group engages in, it provokes real personal responsibility within a group. It is both inter- and intrapersonal in aspect. And it lets learners' imaginations and interpretations fly.

## Alternatives

We can organise a running dictation activity. Put one copy of the poem at the front of the class and groups send representatives up to the front to take back the poem, line by line, by reading and remembering the individual lines in sequence. Learners seem to almost co-create the poem's meaning and form!

## Online/virtual variations

On classroom online platforms you can give the learners the poem in the chat/text box or share the screen. They are then grouped in different 'rooms' to discuss how they can perform it – given the limitations of the situation, and that only one person can speak at a time. Nevertheless, different members of a group can act out/mime while someone else is speaking.

### Where to find poems

You can search online for collections of poems for the classroom. Three of my (UK) favourites are: *I am the Seed that Grew the Tree* edited by Fiona Waters and Frann Preston-Gannon (Nosy Crow Ltd.) for children, *Poems to Live Your Life By*, chosen and illustrated by Chris Riddell (Pan Macmillan) and *Poems on the Underground* (Penguin UK).

## 42

**Poetry learning**

> Learners learn a poem by heart.

Learning by heart sounds like an unlikely activity to use in a collection of communicative activities, yet it is a whole-language process in which learners' own individual communicative skill is exploited to its maximum. It has been part of education for as long as anyone can remember.

1 Read learners a poem. Read it twice, clearly and at an appropriate speed. (I have frequently used *Everyone Sang* by Siegfried Sassoon for this activity at the B2 level or above. See **41** for suggestions about where to find appropriate poems.) Tell learners that you are going to give them a copy of the poem. Don't tell them what they are going to do with it.

2 Give each learner their own individual copy of the poem. Tell them that they have ten minutes to learn the poem by heart. (See below for a discussion about meaning-checking.) They will be momentarily shocked by this if you have not done anything like it before. Explain that they can get up and move around if they want. (Some people – I include myself here! – find it easier to learn by heart while walking around.) They can say the poem aloud, but not loudly. They can learn it using their 'inner voice' or any other technique they wish. Should we check learners' understanding of the poem before they start learning by heart? I am not in favour of this, provided the poem is well chosen. Learning a poem by heart under pressure makes learners process the language in a much more intense and engaged way (trying to work out how it sounds, rhythm and possible meanings, etc.) before we get to stage 7. It is worth trying!

3 Set the timer. Try not to distract anyone but keep watching them all, ready to encourage anyone who doesn't seem to be on task. Ten minutes has been enough in the groups of B2/C1 learners I have worked with using the Sassoon poem (see above). Everything depends on the level of the learners and the poem.

4   When the time limit expires, ask for quiet and give everyone a few seconds to relax.
5   Tell everyone to turn their paper face down. Ask for a volunteer to try and say the poem by heart. Give them time to try and remember – get over stumbles and mistakes, etc. If the learner grinds to a complete halt (it's easy to do!), ask the others to help them. Remember to go back to the first learner to give them the opportunity to complete the poem.
6   Repeat the process with another learner. You can do this as many times as it continues to engage the class. Each time the poem will be better memorised.
7   When the activity is finished, learners in groups can discuss how the activity felt. You can then talk about the poem itself and clear up and discuss meanings and interpretations. (You can search online for information.)

## Why it works for me

Who would have thought an activity as old as education itself could have such a communicative payoff! A combination of the intra-personal, inner voice, interrogation of image and meaning, and learning under pressure ensures this activity's inclusion here.

## Alternatives

We can mix this activity with a re-ordering task. In this version, learners are given individual lines to commit to memory and then put in groups where each line is represented (see **24**).

## Online/virtual variations

This is one of the activities that are difficult to replicate with the same immediate 'feeling' online. However, we can put the poem up on a shared screen for ten minutes and ask learners to learn from there. Of course, we must make sure that everyone is appropriately muted.

## 43

# First draft of history

Learners role play TV/online reporters 'in the field' speaking to the show's anchor in the studio. They describe what is going on around them.

Journalists, it is often said, write the first draft of history, a remark often attributed to Philip L. Graham, the publisher of the Washington Post, though the remark almost certainly predates him! This activity uses that idea to create an imaginative role play.

1   Ask learners to think about the news on TV. Get them to describe what usually happens: the newsreader speaks directly to the camera; we watch a video report; people talk about the weather; and – the point of this activity – the newsreader/anchor talks to journalists clutching their microphones and standing before a camera as the newsreader/anchor asks questions. Explain that this is the focus of the activity they are going to take part in.

2   Have learners focus on the kinds of questions that the newsreader might ask the reporter. (This will depend on the learners' level, of course.) These questions might include:
    *Where are you? What's the mood? What is everyone doing? What's going to happen? What are people saying?*
    You may want to make your own list before you use the activity so that you are ready with your suggestions.

3   Now have learners think about the kinds of things the reporter might say. These could include:
    *Behind me/around me there are/I can see ...*
    *I talked to someone from the X party/group and she told me ...*
    *It feels very peaceful/dangerous ...*
    *Experts are saying that ...*

4   Tell learners they are witnessing a parade to celebrate carnival (or some other parade-like activity). Give them a bit of time to note down what might be going on. Talk about some of the vocabulary they might use. You can make suggestions here if you want to.

5  Put learners in pairs and allow them to practise the role play, where one of them is the studio anchor person (see 2 above) and the other is the reporter (see 3 above). Go round the pairs listening, helping and making appropriate suggestions.

6  Now go to the main activity. Learners choose from the various possibilities such as a ceremony (like the Oscars); the public launch of a ship, craft, product; a demonstration; a famous battle from history; etc.

7  Put learners into groups and, with the event they have chosen, they talk about what might be happening, what words they need, who might be there.

8  Now learners practise the TV broadcast in pairs. When they have had a chance to do this, some pairs can perform for the rest of the class. It might help if you do some physical moving of class furniture. The news reader/anchor can be seated behind a table and the reporter can be standing. Finally, you can offer feedback with commendations and suggestions for how things could be improved.

## Why it works for me

I love this 'real-world-with-a-twist' activity. Its TV simulation play-acting is one that all learners can relate to. As learners hear the different 'broadcasts', their linguistic processes and, hopefully, enjoyment becomes more sophisticated.

## Alternatives

We can extend this activity so that the 'on-the-spot' reporter actually interviews some people around them. They can ask, 'How long have you been here?' 'Why did you come today?'

## Online/virtual variations

This activity feels like it is tailor-made for the online environment. If learners are separated by space – whether in different houses or different countries even – it adds authenticity to the occasion. We can discuss the language from stages 2 and 3 with the whole group. We can put learners in breakout pairs to practise, or, if we don't want to organise that, we can practise with the whole group before having two people do the role play while the others watch.

# F: Activities in sequences

This section shows how activities can be threaded through longer sequences – stretching over more than one lesson, sometimes. In such sequences, communication activities play their part (a very important one) in the construction of a language and topic journey.

# Film a scene from a movie    44

Learners write a movie scene (or series of scenes), rehearse it and then film it.

I once met a teacher in Colombia (Felipe Rodríguez) who told me, on camera, about a movie project his teenage learners had put together, finally filming the whole thing in a wood behind their school. It was, he said, 'wicked' – British slang back then to denote great success. And in 2018, I visited a primary school in Norwich (UK) with a group of French primary teachers. We saw a film the children had made themselves about Black Shuck, the notorious devil from East Anglian folk stories. The benefits from both projects – and more like them from different groups of learners and teachers – are many and profound.

The whole sequence gives learners many opportunities in and outside normal class time to communicate because of their shared goal.

This is an extended and more complex version of 40.

1   In groups, learners discuss (a) their favourite movies/their favourite movie genres and then (b) decide on the kind of movie they would like to film. Go round the groups making suggestions and helping them with the discussions.
2   The groups work out a basic story for the movie they would make (of which they will do just one scene). They might want to search online for typical movie plots. They decide on some characters from their movie – who they are, what they are like, etc. Use this stage to feed in language related to character and appearance.
3   Ask learners to identify a scene from their story that they think would be a good one to film. They start by deciding who is there, where they are, and what their relationships are to one another. They then move on to think about how the characters are feeling at this point (referring to their decisions about character in stage 2). Finally, they decide on what will happen in the scene, create a storyboard and start to put together the dialogue and the scene directions. They can role play the scene before they start writing it.

4 Encourage learners to do several drafts of their script. For each draft, ask them to review their writing and look for better ways of saying things and spot and correct mistakes. While they are doing this, circulate and offer suggestions.

5 Now ask learners to assign roles. Who will play the characters in the scene? Who will direct the scene and make decisions about what the characters do? Who will be the camera operator?

6 The characters rehearse their scene while the director listens, makes suggestions and leads a discussion about aspects of filming (e.g., camera angles, sound effects, etc.).

7 The filming takes place. It may take a few attempts, of course.

8 Groups now show their videos to the rest of the class and people say what they liked and, maybe, suggest ways to expand the scenes.

**Why it works for me**

When learners get behind this activity, they give considerable attention to language, which is pored over and repeated (purposefully). The inter-group interaction is what communication is all about.

**Alternatives**

We can have learners create and film their own episodes of a TV series they are all fond of. They can 'borrow' characters from something they have read or seen. It is useful if we help them to focus their scenes/episodes on realities they are all likely to be familiar with.

**Online/virtual variations**

It's very difficult to film together when you are geographically separate, of course. However, learners can create their scene and record it. And like many projects (theatrical and musical) during the Coronavirus lockdowns, different learners can send in their own filming of a part of the scene which can then be threaded together into a whole.

> **Learners have communicative interactions in preparation for a summary of opinions for a survey.**

What I like about opinion surveys is that they can be used at any level. Even at the A1 level, 'Do you like bananas?' can lead to, 'Ten people in the class like bananas.' The procedure I am going to describe here (and which Philip Harmer used in his classes) is appropriate for learners in groups of ten or more at the B2 or C1 level. This kind of activity is also appropriate for, e.g., IELTS exam preparation – where the results of the survey can be written up.

1 Discuss topics that might interest learners – and which have the potential to engage them. What topic would they like to find out their classmates' opinions on?
2 Ask learners, individually, to formulate the questions they would like to ask. As an example, a learner might select UFOs (unidentified flying objects) as their topic (or you might use this as an example topic). Tell them to think of detailed questions which go beyond simple *yes/no* questions. On the chosen topics of UFOs, you might prompt learners to come up with questions like, 'What are your reasons for (not) believing in UFOs?' 'Why do you think people talk about UFOs so much?' 'Have you ever seen a UFO or a programme about UFOs? Tell me about it?' 'What explains the phenomena of people's fascination with UFOs, do you think?'
3 While learners are formulating their questions, go round the class and offer constructive feedback.
4 Now put learners in pairs. Tell them there is a time limit – say, four minutes – for each conversation. They interview the other learner in their pair and take notes of their answers (or record them).
5 When four minutes are up, the pairs swap roles of interviewer and interviewee for another four minutes. Learners now make new pairs and repeat the process. They do this until everyone in the class has worked in different pairs. While the activity is going on, go round the group offering light-touch feedback.

6 Finally, ask individual learners to collate all the answers they have received. They can make notes to prepare to give an oral presentation (see **47**). Go round and offer constructive feedback.

7 In this and subsequent lessons, individual learners present their findings. The other learners now have the opportunity/obligation to comment and ask questions.

8 When the activity is finished, both you and the learners can make comments about the presentations they have watched, with an emphasis on what they liked about those presentations.

## Why it works for me

This is 'real-life' communication! The preparation of the survey questions, the interviews themselves and the reporting of them ensure satisfying and effective purposeful repetition, attention to meaning in context, and authentic interaction.

## Alternatives

The ideal kind of surveys involve learners interviewing people in 'real' conversations outside the classroom (as when I was questioned, once, by a couple of teenager learners of English outside the Museo de Antropologia in Mexico City). There are obvious safeguarding issues of course, but once overcome, the excitement of having these real-life interactions cannot be overstated.

In an A1 or A2 class, learners make charts with, say, a list of foods and class names. They go round the class asking, 'Do you like bananas? Do you like beetroot? Do you like tomatoes?' etc. and then report back their findings.

## Online/virtual variations

Many people use written online survey programs to gather information, and that can lead to oral presentations, of course. But we want learners to communicate orally with others. We can set up breakout rooms on a rotating basis (setting a time limit for each interview). We can ask friends and colleagues if they will agree to be interviewed online by learners. We can ask them to interview each other, etc.

Learners prepare for and take part in a formal debate.

We are all familiar with the concept of debating, whether in politics, for example, discussion or university or school activities. The English classroom is no different – just a bit more challenging! We have to be available to help (see stage 3).

In a formal debate, opposing teams put together arguments and argue against each other before a vote is taken on who has made their arguments most effectively.

1　Tell learners that they are going to take part in a formal debate and explain the rules and procedure: two opposing teams speak for and against a motion/proposition. This is how it works: a proposer from team A speaks for five minutes. Then an opposer from team B speaks for the same amount of time. A second proposer from team A speaks for three minutes, trying to answer team B's first speaker. Now a second speaker from team B speaks, trying to answer team A's first speaker. Now, at this point, members of the 'audience' can make their comments on what they have heard and ask questions. Next, the second speaker from team A makes a short summarising comment and the second speaker from team B does the same. Finally, the main speakers make their closing summaries and appeal for the audience's vote. The audience now vote for or against the proposition based on what they have heard.

2　Divide the class into two teams, A and B. They have to consider a proposition such as: 'The rise of social media has done more harm than good.' Team A has to discuss reasons that they could use to support that proposition. Team B has to marshal arguments about why, on the contrary, social media has done more good than harm. Explain that these arguments do not have to depend on the group members' personal beliefs. Instead, the idea is to think of arguments to support the point of view they are arguing for, whatever they themselves might feel about it.

3 Set a time limit for their discussions. Help teams with language difficulties and suggest ways of saying things.

4 Now each group selects a proposer (main) speaker and seconder. The rest of the group now detach themselves from their team so that they can be the audience where they are free to react and speak as themselves. They make their own evaluation based on their feelings and the speakers' performances.

5 Appoint someone to take charge of the debate. They have to say who speaks when and keep a strict control on the time they have been given. Some teachers prefer to take on this role themselves so that they can ensure the debate's smooth running and offer encouragement when the pace or the enthusiasm sags.

6 The debate now takes place. When the four initial speakers have made their arguments, set a time limit for audience comments and questions.

7 When the debate has finished, get the audience to vote.

8 Conduct feedback with the class. Who did they think spoke best or made the most effective points? You may wish to add your own comments and, perhaps, pick out any language you want to highlight and improve.

### Why it works for me

What has always appealed to me about this activity is that learners have to really listen to others and respond accordingly – quite apart from finding the right words to express their own meanings. Debates have so much of what we are looking for!

### Alternatives

A much shorter version – which does not involve such a detailed sequence – is *Tennis match* (see **16.**)

### Online/virtual variations

Online debates miss some of the features of physically shared space, of course. But learners can still prepare in groups and deliver their speeches – and be questioned. This demands a clear online turn-taking protocol. Inbuilt emojis on the platform can be used for voting.

> Learners work in groups to prepare and deliver an oral presentation supported by whatever visuals, media or props they need.

Project work has always been part of teachers' repertoires. It demands a sustained attention span and dedication from learners, including research and planning. Since the arrival of online access, project work has become more feasible.

1 Before the lesson or lessons, select a topic for the learners to work on. It can be anything from the typical 'Sites of interest in our town/ city', to 'How mobile devices have affected real life conversation', 'How the world is combatting the climate crisis,' or 'Fashion through the ages'. Alternatively, you can ask learners to choose their own topics or give them a range of alternatives which they can choose from. Decide on how long the students will have; a 60-minute sequence demands quick thought and pressured communication; a longer sequence, over more than one lesson, will give learners time to conduct face-to-face interviews, take pictures or do more in-depth research.

2 Tell the learners that they are going to work in groups to prepare a presentation for the rest of the class. Explain that each individual learner must be an active participant in the presentation (see also **41**) and that they can use any tools or media to help them make their presentation.

3 Put learners in groups – probably not smaller than three or bigger than five or six. Offer them the topic(s) you have chosen (see 1 above). If you have offered alternatives, give them a few moments to discuss their choice.

4 Offer learners stages that might help them plan their presentations: for example, they can come up with initial ideas about topic and structure. They decide how they are going to research the topic (online, using the library or face-to-face interviews, etc.).

5   When the groups have collected all their data, they try and put it into some sequence. While they are doing this (and with all the stages from 3 onwards), go round the groups, checking on their progress, offering suggestions, and helping with any language issues that may come up. In particular, you may need to encourage learners to limit their focus if, as sometimes happens, they try to do too much.

6   Learners now put their presentations together and practise what they are going to say. Remind them that each one must play a part in the presentations.

7   Groups present to the rest of the class. Each person listening is asked to write down at least one question.

8   When a group finishes, get the listeners to ask their questions ensuring, over the course of this stage, that every learner asks at least one question.

9   Together with other learners, give feedback on what you have heard and help learners to make improvements so that they can re-do the presentation. Such task repetition is both satisfying for them and valuable for learning.

## Why it works for me

It's the inter-group co-operation and work on repeated language elements that make this such an effective activity. I love the sense of individual responsibility within the group that happens.

## Alternatives

Learners can listen in groups of three. One says three things they liked about the presentation; the next asks three questions about what they have heard and seen and the third says three things they would express differently or have a different opinion about. The presenting group then looks at their presentation again with a view to making it better.

## Online/virtual variations

This sequence can be put together by groups of learners online. They can be in contact with each other – operating in their online groups. They can prepare their presentations and the presentation media they wish to use. They present to their colleagues online, one by one, whilst using screenshare for the media they have chosen.

Groups identify a job and design interview questions for it. Then they hold the interviews.

Going for an interview is something that all of us have to do in our lives, sometimes many times! This activity thus has a useful dual focus: language improvement and life-skill training.

1  Ask learners what questions they would expect to meet if they went for a job interview – for just about any job. These might be things (for a B2 class) like, 'Why do you want this job?' 'What qualities would you bring to this job if you were successful?' 'Why do you think you are suited for this post' 'Do you have any questions for us?' etc. For lower levels questions might be, e.g., 'Why are you good for this job/post?' or 'Why are you the right person for this job?' etc.

2  Ask the class to select a job that they want to focus on. It is wise to take your own suggestions into the classroom to help them along. The jobs could be anything from fire officer, children's library assistant, supermarket clerk to pilot, waiter, school principal, hairdresser, etc. Tell learners, individually, to choose a job and think about what qualities would be required in such a job.

3  Divide the class into two groups. Each group comes to a decision about one job and then discusses five qualities they will be looking for in a successful applicant. While they are doing this, go to the two groups and make sure they are on task. You may want to give a time limit for the two stages of decision-making (the job and the desirable qualities).

(In large classes, you can set up any number of groups to prepare and enact job interviews. Other learners (candidates) go from group to group. Did each group choose the same person if each group was interviewing for the same job?)

4  Now tell each group to come up with ten questions which they will ask each candidate. The questions should not only elicit answers about the candidate's character but also about how well they match

the qualities that were identified in stage 3. Check over the questions and help with minor suggestions to make them more effective.

5 When the questions are ready, tell each group what the other group's choice of job is and what desirable qualities they are looking for. Groups now have a chance to predict what questions the other team will ask them. Give them a chance to discuss how they might answer them.

6 A learner from each group goes to the other group and is interviewed by them for the job they have decided on. Tell interviewing groups that they should be welcomed, offered a seat, given introductions, etc., just as in a life-outside-the-classroom interview. The members of the interviewing group take notes of the answers the interviewees give. When the first interview is done, two more learners swap groups and the process is repeated, with exactly the same questions.

7 The activity continues until all learners have been interviewed. Now each group discusses who they will choose and why. The results are announced!

8 Lead a discussion with the whole class. What did they learn from the activity? What did they like and not like about it? Which of their questions were successful for helping them make their choice and which were not? Which questions did the interviewees find easy/not so easy, etc?

## Why it works for me

The question preparation and the interviews are incredibly language rich and the decisions – because they are based on the interviews themselves – ensure authentic communication and real attention to language.

## Alternatives

Groups can design charts/forms to fill in about each candidate to help them in their post-interview discussions.

## Online/virtual variations

Many interviews take place online in real life. All we have to do is replicate that with our groups going into breakout rooms instead of gathering together in physical space.

Learners create a newspaper/website front page and respond to new stories as they come in.

There is a long tradition in language teaching of simulating the activity in a newsroom where decisions have to be made, headlines created, articles written and changes made, sometimes at the last moment (see stage 8).

This activity can, of course, be compressed into a one-lesson sequence, but it has much more power when it stretches over two or more classes. It becomes as much a learning as a practice activity.

1 Give learners examples of print newspapers and online sites. What you choose will depend on their age and level, of course. Ask them to notice features such as how articles are constructed – an opening paragraph which briefly states the whole 'story', detailed information in the next paragraphs, final paragraph which sums up the story and ends with questions or (what people say) is going to happen next. Have them look at the headlines and see how they are constructed: in print media, grammar words such as articles and auxiliaries are often omitted, for example. Online headlines are often more 'complete', but how and why? Ask learners to look at what stories come first and why. Finally, they can discuss issues such as what photos and other visuals are used and why.

2 Put learners in small groups. Give each group two or three different stories. Depending on their age and level, these can be ones that you invent or adapt. In higher level groups, you can hand round newspapers and/or have them investigate different online news sites. You can assign different sites to different groups. Ask the learners to make notes of all the main stories – but not the headlines, especially. You should also find, adapt or write some appropriate stories to feed in as 'late-arriving news' at stage 8.

3 Now make new groups by moving one or two learners from the original groups. (If it is a smaller class, these next stages can all be done as a whole class activity.)

4   Ask learners to share the stories they have found. While they are discussing them, they should start to think of which ones are the most important.

5   Now tell learners how many stories should fit on their front page. Tell them to choose which ones they will include. Depending on their age and level you can give them word limits for each article – and other constraints to help them formulate their pieces.

6   Learners now write their articles following, as far as the possible, the models they came across in stage 1. While they are doing this you can go round offering support and advice.

7   Now ask learners to write the headlines.

8   Give learners time to design their pages. The learners who have the best digital skills should do the layout and design while the others offer their opinions and suggestions. At this stage – depending on the level of the class and the time available – you can introduce some late-arriving stories. The students will have to decide whether to include them or not, and how this will affect the layout of the front page.

9   When learners have finished their front page, they can show them to the whole class who then evaluate them and, if you think this is appropriate, choose their favourite.

## Why it works for me

*Front page* is an exciting 'hands-on' activity which involves reading (and listening/watching), design, and crucially (which is where the face-to-face communication comes in), discussion and decision-making. Best of all, the learners have something to show for it when it is over.

## Alternatives

You can use the same basic procedure to recreate a radio or TV newsroom. Learners have to choose the stories which will be aired, what order they will be presented in, and what words the newsreader will use. Once again, we can feed in late-arriving news, and we can have them make the programme after choosing camera operatives, newscaster, etc. (see also **43**). We can substitute other topics (fashion, entertainment, sport etc.) instead of general news if we wish.

## Online/virtual variations

This activity works extremely well online since it is exactly how many print and online media organisations operate anyway.

Learners prepare to interview a visitor to their virtual class including writing letters of invitation and questions. They research the visitor's life and occupation. After the visit – in which they interview their guest – they write thank you letters and reflect on what they have learned.

Preparing to interview a visitor to a class (research, invitations, question preparation, etc.); interviewing the visitor; summarising the interview later; writing thank you mails; etc. These are all part of a rich communicative sequence. I am going to describe such a sequence used by An Croenen Brutsaert with her online learners. I am very grateful to her for letting me describe her lesson(s) here. The sequence was provoked by a song called *The President Sang Amazing Grace* by the folk artist Zoe Mulford – who then became the class 'visitor'. The song details the visit of then-US president Barack Obama to Charleston, South Carolina in June 2015 to commemorate nine victims of a white supremacist murderer.

1　An started by asking her learners to look at a photo of President Barack Obama attending a memorial service in Charleston, South Carolina on June 17, 2015. In breakout rooms, pairs were asked to discuss whether they were surprised that the photo is from a funeral. They were told that it shows the president singing the song *Amazing Grace* about forgiveness, and they were asked to speculate why he would do that – and then to research it online.

2　The learners watched a YouTube video of the event that day.

3　They then did a matching definitions exercise with qualities such as 'introspective', 'empathetic', 'adaptable' and 'resilient' and discussed which qualities a leader should have.

4　The learners were told they were going to meet a folk singer called Zoe Mulford in a few days. They did a fill-in discovery exercise about her and her song.

5　The learners were directed to a video of Mulford singing the song (see below). A glossary was provided for potentially problematic words or phrases.

6  Together the learners wrote a letter of invitation to Zoe Mulford.
   They prepared questions they would like to ask her.
7  In an online session, the learners interviewed Zoe Mulford
   and interacted with the answers she gave. This was the main
   communicative activity at the heart of this sequence.
8  After the interview the learners discussed their reactions to it. They
   were encouraged to write thank you letters to their visitor. One
   student, for example, wrote, 'You are a great person who is able to
   talk about everything with such wisdom and humility.'

## Why it works for me

Nothing can provoke real-life processing and emotional/cognitive
engagement more than this kind of activity with its authentic
communicative interactions and meaningful real-life stories. It is a
fitting last activity sequence for this collection.

## Alternatives

If we can't invite a real person into our virtual classroom, we can
get learners to role play an interview with an imaginary character
or celebrity. It can be good fun to imagine what they might say! Or
they can decide together on questions they would like to ask someone
famous and then imagine what their answers might be.

## Face to face variation

As Laura Edwards pointed out during an online conference in 2020, it
is easier to get someone to agree to be interviewed online than in real
life – it is less disruptive for the interviewee (Edwards 2020). However,
it is surely possible, sometimes, to invite a physical person into the
classroom – anyone the learners might find interesting. They can be a
mystery person and the learners have to find out who they are and *why*
they are interesting. We will need to prepare our visitor for the learners'
language level.

*The President sang Amazing Grace* can be seen and heard at
https://zoemulford.com/the-story-of-the-president-sang-amazing-grace
(accessed 04/12/2020)

Edwards, L. (2020). 'IATEFL Global get together'
https://www.youtube.com/watch?v=zgCzsB1LOkM&t=1393s (accessed 22/12/2020)

# Index